THE
POWER
OF
PAIN

TRANSFORMING SUFFERING
INTO STRENGTH AND SUCCESS

IVAN D. LOZADA

THE POWER OF PAIN

Transforming Suffering into Strength And Success

Copyright © 2025 by Ivan D. Lozada

This book is intended for informational and educational purposes only and should not be considered financial, legal, or investment advice. While every effort has been made to provide accurate and useful insights, investing involves risk, and past performance is no guarantee of future results. Additionally, the market is constantly changing—stock prices, company situations, and economic conditions may have shifted since this book was written. Any examples provided are for illustration only and should not be interpreted as recommendations. Always conduct your own research and consult with a qualified financial professional before making any investment decisions.

CONTENTS

INTRODUCTION

The Paradox of Pain and the Promise of Growth

On a sweltering afternoon in Caracas, I crouched behind a crumbling wall, heart pounding in my chest. Moments earlier, a bomb had exploded under my car. The blast shattered windows and sent shockwaves through the neighborhood. By some miracle, I was unhurt, having been just meters away. Every instinct screamed at me to run, to escape, to avoid any more pain. Yet in that moment of terror, I glimpsed a truth that would reshape my life: this devastating experience would become the catalyst for my purpose, unlocking a destiny far beyond my own survival.

If not for the suffering I endured—the persecution by the Venezuelan regime that forced me into exile and the agonizing loss of my homeland—I might never have discovered the wellspring of strength that later drove me to found DolarToday. What began as a desperate flight from danger evolved into a mission: creating a digital platform that exposed the truth about Venezuela's dictatorship and gave voice to silenced citizens. The bomb that nearly took my life ignited something more powerful within me—a force of resilience that redefined what I thought possible. In that crucible of suffering, I found not just the courage to rebuild my life as a political asylum seeker in the United States, but the resolve to fight for the freedom of the country I was forced to leave behind.

Using my pain is something that goes against the conventions of modern society. Instead, our society has perfected the art of avoiding pain. We chase comfort and shield ourselves from every hurt. We're told to avoid pain at all costs and pursue happiness relentlessly. This instinct served us well in evolution—helping us evade danger and injury. But in our world of constant convenience, this fear of pain has become counterproductive.

Psychologist Brené Brown observed that "When you numb your pain, you also numb your joy." In our rush to medicate, distract, and tune out discomfort, we dull our capacity for happiness and meaning. By avoiding pain, we limit our growth. When we stay within our comfort bubbles, never stretching our limits, we narrow our world and weaken our ability to face life's inevitable challenges. Ironically, we often suffer more from our desperate attempts to avoid pain than from the pain itself.

Here lies the great paradox: Pain is profoundly unpleasant, yet it remains one of our greatest teachers. Nearly every wisdom tradition points to the transformative power of suffering. The ancient Greeks spoke of *pathei mathos*—"learning through suffering." Buddhist doctrine builds around understanding suffering (*dukkha*) as an inescapable reality and seeking wisdom through it. The Bible teaches, "Suffering produces endurance, and endurance produces character, and character produces hope." History and human experience repeatedly show that great strength is often forged in the fires of adversity. Modern psychology confirms what Friedrich Nietzsche pointed out long ago: that which does not kill us can, in many cases, make us stronger.

What if instead of spending our lives running from pain, we turned to face it? What if we embraced our pain and harnessed it? This book argues that pain, rather than being only an experience to dread, can become a powerful catalyst for personal growth and even societal transformation. Pain is not good in itself—no one enjoys suffering—but pain often serves as the portal to resilience, wisdom, and strength that we cannot gain otherwise. As counterintuitive as it sounds, embracing our suffering can unlock our greatest power.

In the pages that follow, we will explore this theme from every angle. We'll begin with an examination of the nature of pain—what science tells us about why we feel pain and how it affects the mind and body. We will see how pain functions not just as a physical sensation but as a psychological and spiritual experience that shapes us.

Next, we'll consider the gift of adversity, looking at history and contemporary stories of individuals who transformed their suffering into strength. We'll delve into teachings from Jesus of Nazareth on suffering, forgiveness, and resilience—not as religious sermonizing, but as universal philosophical insights on finding meaning through unimaginable pain. We will draw on Viktor Frankl's experiences in the Holocaust and the wisdom of Buddhist and Stoic philosophies to understand how humans discover meaning in suffering. We'll survey cutting-edge research in neuroscience and psychology to uncover the science of resilience—how our brains and minds adapt and even thrive after trauma.

Crucially, this book is not just about ideas, but action. In chapter 6, "Practical Strategies for Turning Pain into Power," we will outline concrete, research-backed techniques—mindfulness practices, journaling, reframing thoughts, self-compassion, and more—that anyone can use to convert their own pain into personal power.

Throughout the book, you'll find short first-person anecdotes from my journey as an immigrant and political activist. I'll share how the darkest moments in my life— fleeing political persecution and starting over in a foreign land—eventually fueled my determination and purpose. These stories are brief but written from the heart, showing that this isn't just theory for me; it's deeply personal.

You will also meet a diverse cast of inspirational figures—from Nelson Mandela and Malala Yousafzai to Stephen Hawking, Frida Kahlo, and Oprah Winfrey— real people who endured tremendous suffering and emerged not just intact, but extraordinary. Their lives prove that triumph can rise from tragedy.

Each chapter concludes with Pain-to-Power Exercises—practical activities, reflections, or challenges for applying the concepts to your own life. Think of them as a toolkit for resilience. If you engage with these exercises, you won't just be reading about transforming pain; you'll be doing it. Step by step, you can build your resilience muscles and learn to approach difficulties in a new way.

My tone throughout will be conversational and honest—I'll share vulnerabilities and struggles openly—while providing the most reliable knowledge I can find. Think of it as a heartfelt conversation backed by lived experience and research. By the end, I hope you feel not only convinced that pain can serve a purpose but also equipped and inspired to embrace your own struggles and transform them into strength.

Pain is a universal human experience. There is no life without some suffering. We cannot control when pain enters our lives, but we can control our response to it. Within that response lies our freedom and power. As I've learned through my own journey, the very things that hurt us can become the things that empower us—if we let them. So, as we begin this exploration, I invite you to consider an idea that may feel radical: your pain can be your greatest ally.

Let's discover how.

> *We cannot selectively numb emotions; when we numb the painful emotions, we also numb the positive emotions.*
>
> —Brené Brown

Like a physician who studies an illness before treating it, we need to examine pain itself—what it is, how it functions, and why we feel it—before we can harness its potential.

CHAPTER 1

The Nature of Pain

Understanding Pain—Body, Mind, and Spirit

On that afternoon in Caracas when the bomb exploded under my car, I experienced pain's primal power. The explosion shattered more than just windows—it shattered my sense of safety. This visceral experience taught me that pain, whether physical or emotional, serves as our body's urgent alert system.

However, pain can also serve as a powerful catalyst. "How?" you might ask. Like a physician studying an illness before treating it, we must examine pain itself—what it is, how it functions, and why we feel it—before we can harness its potential. Understanding pain across its physical, emotional, and spiritual dimensions reveals not just how it hurts us, but how it communicates with us and shapes our humanity. In seeing pain clearly, we take our first step toward transforming it.

So, what exactly is pain? The International Association for the Study of Pain defines pain as "an unpleasant sensory and emotional experience associated with actual or potential tissue damage." In other words, pain is not just the sensation in your toe when you stub it; it's also the emotional unpleasantness that comes with it. Pain hurts, by definition.

The Physical Nature of Pain

When you experience physical pain, your body triggers a cascade of neurological and chemical responses. The area of injury releases chemicals that sensitize nerves, an electrical signal shoots up the spinal cord to the brain, and the brain interprets the signal, sending back instructions (like moving your hand away) and creating the feeling of hurt. Remarkably, the brain can even create pain without a physical cause—for example, amputees often feel "phantom limb" pain in a limb that is no longer there. This shows that pain isn't only in our body; it's also in our brain's perception.

Sensory and Affective Components

Pain has two main components, as scientists explain. One is the *sensory component*: where the pain is, how intense it is, and how long it lasts. The second is the *affective component*: how it makes you feel emotionally. That second part is why the same injury can feel more painful when you're scared or upset and less painful when you're calm or distracted. Our mind influences our experience of pain tremendously.

The Overlap of Physical and Emotional Pain

Interestingly, modern neuroscience has found that social or emotional pain and physical pain share similar pathways in the brain. Have you ever felt heartache after a breakup or felt stabbed in the back by a betrayal? These are more than metaphors. Brain imaging studies show that rejection or social exclusion activates the same brain regions that process physical pain. To your brain, being ostracized by peers can hurt like a physical wound. The overlap is so real that taking a painkiller like acetaminophen has been shown in some studies to dull the emotional pain of social rejection (though this is not an advised coping strategy!). This neural overlap tells us something profound: pain is pain, whether it's physical or emotional. The brain doesn't draw a sharp line between a broken bone and a broken heart.

The Invisibility of Emotional Pain

While society readily acknowledges physical pain, we often minimize or misunderstand emotional pain. Yet psychological suffering—grief, loneliness, shame, anxiety, and depression—can be just as intense and debilitating as bodily injury, sometimes more so. Emotional pain doesn't show on an X-ray, but it can hollow out our lives and rob us of joy just the same. In fact, as a survivor of both physical dangers and deep emotional turmoil, I can attest that the bruises you can't see may hurt the longest.

Examples of Emotional Pain

Consider Maria, a woman who lost her mother to cancer. Six months after the funeral, her friends expected her to be over it. They couldn't see her pain, so they assumed it had healed. But each morning, she still woke to that moment of crushing remembrance—her mother was gone. The grief remained raw, a wound reopened daily. Maria's experience illustrates what many of us have felt: emotional pain can linger long after others expect us to move on. The invisibility of such pain often makes it harder to bear, as we suffer in silence while the world continues around us.

Or think about the child who feels the sting of rejection at school—excluded from games, whispered about, left out of birthday parties. This social pain may seem trivial to adults, but research shows it registers in the young brain with the same intensity as physical harm. Some of us carry these emotional wounds from childhood into adulthood, where they shape our relationships and self-image in profound ways. The child who was bullied might grow into an adult who struggles with trust or self-worth, the pain echoing decades later.

The Nature of Emotional Wounds

Psychologists describe emotional pain as a kind of wound to our sense of self. One scientific description calls it "a lasting, unpleasant feeling resulting from the negative appraisal of an inability to obtain something or a loss"—in simpler terms, soul pain that arises when our needs for love, security, or meaning aren't met. Unlike a cut that usually heals with time and care, emotional wounds can fester if ignored.

However, we live in a culture that often encourages us to ignore or escape emotional pain. We tell ourselves to suck it up, move on, or stay positive," sometimes at the expense of acknowledging what hurts. We might use external numbing agents—alcohol, drugs, endless screen time—to drown out sadness or stress. But as mentioned earlier, numbing pain also numbs joy, and it postpones healing.

The Avoidance Trap

Why do we avoid emotional pain so strongly? Quite simply, because it's awful to feel. Emotional pain triggers the same aversion circuits as physical pain, and our brain screams, "Run away!" But where can you run from a pain that lives inside your mind and heart? The strategies that work for physical pain (like medication) don't neatly apply to psychological pain. There is no quick pill to erase a painful memory or the sting of grief. So, many of us develop behaviors to dodge these feelings: we withdraw, we deny the pain, or we seek constant comfort and distraction.

The irony is that the more we flee from emotional pain, the more it seems to pursue us. If you've ever tried not to think about something that upsets you, you know how it can boomerang right back into your thoughts. Psychologists call this the *avoidance trap*, where unaddressed pain often grows in the dark. It's like an infection under the skin—covering it up doesn't cure it, and it might spread. On the other hand, when we acknowledge and face emotional pain, we create an opportunity to understand it and heal. We'll talk much more about this in later chapters on meaning and resilience.

Pain as a Whole-Person Experience

When I fled my country, leaving behind my career and loved ones, the grief manifested as insomnia and persistent tension headaches. My body carried what my heart couldn't process. This is because pain is a whole-person experience. It's physical, emotional, and even social (as anyone who's been the outcast in a group knows). Because pain permeates both body and soul, overcoming pain—or rather, transforming our relationship with it—must involve both body and soul.

Philosophical Perspectives: Why Pain Matters

Philosophers and spiritual teachers have grappled with the question of pain for millennia: Why do we suffer? Is there a purpose to pain, or is it purely an evil to eliminate? While the answers differ, most philosophies acknowledge pain as an inseparable part of the human condition—and often, as an indispensable agent of growth. In this convergence of ancient wisdom and modern insight, we uncover a radical truth: pain is not merely a burden to endure but a universal crucible through which humanity's deepest capacities are forged.

The Stoic philosophers of ancient Greece and Rome, like Epictetus and Seneca, believed in confronting pain with courage and wisdom. They taught that while we can't always control what happens to us (the Stoics themselves endured exile, illness, and injury), we can control our attitude. Stoicism frames pain as an opportunity to practice virtue—patience, endurance, fortitude. Seneca famously said, "We are more often frightened than hurt, and we suffer more in imagination than in reality."

In Stoic thought, pain is real, but our fear of pain can amplify it far beyond the actual harm. This insight suggests that by addressing our anticipatory anxiety and catastrophic thinking about pain, we can significantly reduce our suffering. The Stoics didn't seek out pain, but they also didn't consider it the worst evil—being a coward or unjust was far worse. In their view, a person refined by trials is like gold tested in fire (to paraphrase Seneca: fire tests gold, suffering tests brave men).

In Eastern philosophies, we see another perspective. Buddhism squarely centers on the reality of suffering. The very first of the Buddha's Four Noble Truths states that life contains *dukkha*, often translated as "suffering" or "unsatisfactoriness." Rather than denying pain, Buddhism teaches us to acknowledge it and understand its causes (such as attachment and aversion). Paradoxically, by accepting the existence of pain, we can begin to free ourselves from it. The Buddha taught that unrecognized desire and aversion keep us trapped in suffering, but through mindfulness and compassion, we can alleviate our mental anguish. In Buddhist practice, pain becomes a teacher—when you meditate, for example, and feel an ache in your legs, instead of instantly shifting to comfort, you observe the sensation with curiosity. You learn that pain is ever-changing, not permanent; you learn you can experience discomfort without panicking or resenting it. Over time, this builds immense mental resilience.

Further, there's a saying often associated with Buddhism: "Pain is inevitable, suffering is optional." While that might be an oversimplification, it captures the idea that while we all encounter pain, our mindset can greatly reduce the additional suffering we inflict on ourselves through resistance and fear.

From a psychological standpoint, modern positive psychology concurs that facing challenges (including painful ones) is key to growth. Later we'll delve into the concept of post-traumatic growth, but briefly: studies have found that many people report positive transformations after surviving tragedies—a greater appreciation of life, stronger relationships, newfound personal strength, spiritual development, and a redefined sense of purpose. In one study, as many as 89 percent of trauma survivors said they experienced at least one aspect of personal growth in the aftermath. This doesn't mean trauma is "good," but it means human beings often have an astounding capacity to turn pain into power. The seeds of that power lie in how we perceive and respond to the pain.

In short, pain is an integral part of being alive. It is a warning signal and teacher, and it is both a physical event and an emotional experience. Society may tempt us to view pain only as an enemy—to medicate it, ignore it, or banish it from our thoughts. But as we're beginning to see, avoiding pain at all costs can cost us dearly in growth. If we can instead understand pain's nature and listen to its messages, we set the stage for resilience. Pain tells us when something is wrong—physically in our body or metaphorically in our life. By listening to pain, we can begin to make changes, whether that means pulling our hand from the flame or pulling our life onto a new course.

In the next chapter, we will shift from understanding pain itself to exploring how adversity can actually be a gift in disguise. Before we do, take a moment to consider your own experiences of pain. What has physical pain taught you about your limits or priorities? What has emotional pain revealed about what you value or who you are? You may find that in hindsight, some of your deepest insights and strengths were born from your hardest moments. Keep those in mind, as they will illuminate the path forward.

Pain-to-Power Exercises – Chapter 1

1. Body Scan Awareness: Find a quiet moment to sit and perform a gentle body scan. Starting from your toes and moving upward, notice any areas of physical discomfort or tension. Rather than immediately shifting to get comfortable, practice observing the sensation. How does it actually feel (sharp, dull, throbbing, tight)? Breathe slowly and imagine sending your breath to that area. This exercise builds your ability to face physical discomfort with calm awareness. Practicing it regularly strengthens your capacity to be present with discomfort without being overwhelmed by it, laying a foundation for changing your relationship with pain.

2. Journaling on Past Pain: Take ten minutes to write about a painful experience (physical or emotional) that you remember well. Describe what happened and, importantly, what you felt. Then write about what this pain taught you. Did any good come out of it? For example, did a health scare lead you to live healthier, or did a heartbreak eventually teach you something about yourself or what you want in life? This reflection helps extract meaning from past pain and reinforces the idea that suffering can lead to insight. Review your writing to notice patterns in how you've grown through difficulty, building confidence in your ability to transform future challenges.

3. Reframe the Narrative: Pick a minor physical discomfort you feel today (a headache, sore feet, etc.) or a minor emotional discomfort (boredom, mild anxiety). Practice a simple reframing: instead of thinking, "I hate this pain," tell yourself, "This pain is a signal or teacher." Ask yourself, "What is it signaling?" A headache might signal you need rest or hydration; anxiety might signal that something in your life needs attention. By interpreting pain as useful information, you reduce the fear of it and feel more in control. Practice this reframing daily for one week with whatever minor discomforts arise, noticing how this perspective shift gradually changes your automatic response to uncomfortable sensations.

Now that we understand pain's purpose, let's shift our perspective to view adversity not merely as something to endure but as a catalyst that brings unexpected gifts. While the previous chapter explained what pain is, the next reveals what it can do for us when approached with the right mindset.

CHAPTER 2

The Gift of Adversity

How Challenges Shape Us and Why We Need Them

In my first year in America, I stood in a supermarket aisle, overwhelmed yet safe from persecution. My English faltered, and my savings were thin. Counting unfamiliar coins for milk and bread, tears of frustration burned my eyes. "How did I end up here?" I wondered. I had been a lieutenant and activist in Venezuela; now, I was an immigrant stocking shelves to feed my family. Yet in this crucible of adversity, something remarkable began to emerge. The very challenges that felt humiliating were awakening new abilities in me—humility, yes, but also resourcefulness, determination, and empathy for others facing hardship.

It's a bold claim to call adversity a gift. After all, challenges usually involve pain, loss, or struggle. We don't wish misfortune on anyone, including ourselves. Yet life, by its very nature, will present us with adversity. And when it comes, we have two choices: let it break us or let it make us. This chapter explores the second choice—how to recognize the hidden gifts that hardship carries and how history and real lives demonstrate that our struggles can become our superpowers.

Adversity as Teacher and Catalyst

Think of the toughest experience you've endured in your life. Perhaps it was an illness, the death of a loved one, a failure or public embarrassment, a period of financial stress, or a deep betrayal. At the time, it likely felt purely negative, something you wished would end as soon as possible. But in hindsight, did it change you in some lasting way? This question unveils a universal truth: every trial harbors the seeds of transformation.

Many people find that hardships teach them lessons they might never have learned otherwise. Adversity inevitably forces us to adapt, find creative solutions, and build strengths we didn't know we had. It can cut through trivial matters and clarify what truly matters, increase our empathy and compassion for others, and shape our character into a masterpiece of resilience and wisdom.

I remember the first job interview I had in the United States. My hands trembled as I sat across from the manager of a home improvement store, clutching my résumé—hastily translated and sparse on American experience. When asked about my qualifications, I stumbled over English words, mortified at how my education and military background seemed to vanish in this new context. The manager's expression remained neutral, but I felt diminished, reduced to my broken language and unfamiliarity with American customs.

I didn't get that job. Walking back to the bus stop, rejection stinging sharply, I questioned everything: my decision to leave my motherland, my ability to provide for my family, my very identity. But that evening, I sat down and did something I hadn't done before—I reached out to other immigrants from my land who had successfully integrated into American society. Their stories of initial struggles followed by gradual triumph gave me both practical tips and emotional strength. The very next week, better prepared and slightly more confident, I secured a position at another store. That first rejection, painful as it was, pushed me to build a network of support that would prove invaluable throughout my transition.

As one tour guide in South Africa poignantly said of Nelson Mandela's twenty-seven-year imprisonment, "If we didn't have apartheid, we wouldn't have had Nelson Mandela." The great leader who emerged from prison—wise, patient, and forgiving—was forged by that extreme adversity.

Psychologists sometimes talk about the concept of the *adversity quotient*, which, like IQ or EQ, posits that individuals differ in how well they withstand and use adversity. Regardless of what one thinks about quantifying it, we can intuitively see that people respond to hardship very differently. Some crumble, while others seem to draw strength from struggle like steel tempered in fire. What makes the difference? Often, it's mindset and support (topics we will explore in later chapters on resilience science and strategies). But one thing is clear: without any adversity at all, a person never truly knows their own strength. Muscles do not grow without resistance; similarly, our psychological and spiritual muscles don't grow without life testing them.

The Danger of Comfort: Why Ease Can Make Us Fragile

In fact, a life of endless ease can leave us unprepared and fragile. Modern comfort, while wonderful in many ways, has a side effect: it can make us less resilient. If a child is always shielded from every disappointment or failure, they may struggle to cope in adulthood when something inevitably doesn't go their way. If we avoid every risk of hurt, we also avoid opportunities to learn courage. Adversity, unpleasant as it is, teaches us to bounce back and improvise. It reveals a reservoir of endurance we might not tap into otherwise.

Consider the phenomenon of helicopter parenting, where well-meaning adults hover over children, removing every obstacle from their path. Research has shown that children raised this way often develop anxiety and poor coping skills when facing challenges later in life, as they never developed the emotional muscles needed to handle disappointment or setbacks. Similarly, in my home country, I observed families of privilege whose children were cocooned from Venezuela's harsh realities. When the political crisis erupted and those comforts vanished, many struggled profoundly with the adjustment, while children from more modest backgrounds—who had always needed to be resourceful—often adapted more readily.

There's a term for this in biology and psychology: *stress inoculation*. Just as a vaccine exposes you to a small, manageable dose of a virus to build your immunity, life's smaller trials can build your resilience for bigger challenges ahead. Facing moderate stresses—a difficult project, an athletic competition, a move to a new city—can make you more confident and skilled at coping. Conversely, having too little challenge can leave you surprisingly helpless when a tough day finally arrives. As one *Psychology Today* article stated: "Without sufficient stress, people lose their ability to cope with adversity and become less resilient. The key is finding that sweet spot of challenge—enough to grow, but not so much as to overwhelm." (We'll revisit this concept of optimal stress in the resilience science chapter.)

This perspective reshapes how we might view life's difficulties. That project that keeps you up at night, the relationship conflict that forces difficult conversations, the financial setback that requires creative budgeting—these challenges are developing your capacity to withstand greater storms. They are, in essence, strengthening your life muscles.

Historical and Contemporary Examples of Triumph Over Trials

To truly see the gift of adversity, it helps to look at concrete examples. History is full of stories of individuals who not only survived hardship but also transformed it into legacy and achievement. Let's briefly visit a few, though we'll explore many of these more in depth in chapter 9.

Thomas Edison, the famed inventor, was once asked about the thousands of failed experiments he had before inventing a practical light bulb. He famously replied, "I have not failed. I've just found ten thousand ways that won't work." Each "failure" was actually a step forward, gathering knowledge. Without the adversity of so many flops, the eventual triumph might not have been possible. Edison's story shows adversity fostering perseverance and innovation.

Helen Keller became deaf and blind as a toddler due to an illness. The world for her could have been closed, dark, and silent, yet her adversity became her impetus to connect deeply with others in new ways. With the help of a dedicated teacher, Keller not only learned to communicate but went on to become an author and activist, inspiring millions with her story of resilience. She once said, "Although the world is full of suffering, it is also full of the overcoming of it." Her life embodies that overcoming.

The Great Depression in the 1930s was a period of massive adversity for society: unemployment, poverty, and uncertainty. But it also gave rise to an entire generation that learned frugality, innovation, and community solidarity. Many who grew up in that era developed an inner strength and resourcefulness—the so-called "Greatest Generation" that would go on to face World War II. Out of economic pain came lessons in endurance and a resolve to build a better future.

For a more contemporary example, consider J. K. Rowling, who wrote the first Harry Potter book as a single mother on welfare, battling depression after a divorce and her mother's death. She has described that period as being "as poor as it is possible to be in modern Britain without being homeless." Yet those difficult years gave her the story that would captivate millions. Rowling has said that "rock bottom became the solid foundation on which I rebuilt my life." Her adversity—financial struggle, grief, and rejection from publishers—became the fertile ground from which her creativity and determination blossomed.

My homeland's story offers another example. In recent decades, my birth country has faced profound adversity: economic collapse, political turmoil, and scarcity of basic needs. It has been an extraordinarily painful time for its citizens. Yet, amidst this hardship, I have seen people awaken to activism, communities band together, and individuals discover their capacity to survive and help one another.

In fact, that is what prompted the birth of my website, DolarToday. It emerged from chaos when the truth was being stifled. As hyperinflation ravaged the economy, government censorship blocked citizens from knowing the real value of their money. I still remember the adrenaline rush of our first publication—my fingers hovering over the keyboard before uploading the actual black market exchange rate, knowing I was crossing a line that couldn't be uncrossed. If my country had remained stable and free, I might never have found this calling. When the regime later dragged us into US courts, hoping to silence us from abroad, their intimidation backfired. Each threat and legal challenge only confirmed why our work mattered. We weren't just publishing numbers; we were preserving economic reality when everything else had become propaganda. The harder they fought to shut us down, the more certain we became of our purpose.

Adversity drew something out of me and many others: a fierce desire for freedom and justice and creativity in finding ways to fight for it (even from exile, even from a Home Depot in Alabama, where one of my roles was decidedly less glamorous than my former life!).

Adversity as a Clarifier of Purpose and Values

Adversity can also clarify purpose. When life is easy, we may drift or take things for granted. When life knocks us down, we're forced to decide what we really stand for and what we're willing to fight for. Consider someone like Malala Yousafzai, the Pakistani girl who was shot by the Taliban for insisting on girls' right to education. At the age of fifteen, she faced an adversity most of us can scarcely imagine—an assassination attempt. She could have been paralyzed by fear. Instead, as she recovered, her resolve only grew stronger. "They thought that the bullets would silence us, but they failed," Malala said. "Weakness, fear, and hopelessness died. Strength, power, and courage were born." Her suffering became her source of global voice and influence. By age seventeen, she became the youngest Nobel Peace Prize laureate, using her platform to fight for millions of others. In Malala's story, we see adversity as the furnace that forged an indomitable advocate.

This clarification of purpose through adversity isn't limited to high-profile figures. A friend of mine, Carlos, worked as a successful corporate lawyer in Caracas before the economic collapse. When hyperinflation rendered his salary nearly worthless and political instability threatened his family's safety, he emigrated to Costa Rica with only what he could carry. Unable to practice law in his new country without extensive recertification, he took a job at a call center to support his family.

The adversity of starting over was immense, but it led Carlos to rediscover why he had become a lawyer in the first place—to help people navigate complex systems. Today, he runs a small but growing nonprofit that provides legal guidance to other refugees from my compatriots. "I never would have found this purpose if everything had stayed comfortable," he told me recently. "I had to lose every-thing to remember what really mattered."

What these examples teach us is not that we should seek out adversity recklessly, nor that suffering is somehow "fun." Rather, they show that when adversity comes, it carries potential—the potential to awaken latent abilities, strengthen resolve, spark innovation, and bring people together. Challenges force change, and while change can be scary, it's also the only way we grow.

Reframing Challenges as Opportunities

One practical way to start seeing the gift in adversity is to reframe our thoughts when we encounter a challenge. The next time you're faced with a difficulty—big or small—try to catch your inner dialogue. It might be saying, "This is awful, I can't handle this," or, "Why is this happening to me?" That's natural. But see if you can add another perspective: ask yourself, "What is this challenge teaching me?" or, "How might this make me stronger or wiser?" In other words, look for the potential gift.

For instance, losing a job is extremely stressful. But some people later say it was the push they needed to pursue a different career they loved or learn new skills. A painful breakup can eventually lead to greater self-awareness and to finding a more compatible partner down the line. Again, this isn't about Pollyanna-ish positivity; it's about acknowledging that within every loss, there is something to gain, even if it's simply a lesson or a story of survival.

One exercise I often use is to reflect on past adversities that I have already con-verted into gifts. For me, fleeing my nation was harrowing, but it gave me free-dom and a mission. When I struggle with something now, I remind myself, "You've faced worse and grown from it." This boosts my confidence that this, too, shall strengthen me.

The gift of adversity often reveals itself with time. It's okay if you cannot see the silver lining when you are in the throes of hardship. Survival might be all you can manage in the moment—and that's enough. But as you move through it, keep your heart and mind open to the possibility that one day, you may look back on this trial with gratitude for what it taught or gave you.

Let me be clear: this perspective doesn't minimize genuine suffering or suggest that all pain is somehow worth it in the end. Some hardships are devastating, and not every wound yields immediate wisdom. Trauma and injustice are real, and their impacts should never be dismissed. What I suggest instead is that even in our darkest moments, we retain the power to choose how adversity shapes us— whether it will embitter us or ennoble us. We cannot always control what happens to us, but we always have some control over how we respond to it.

The Neuroscience of Growth Through Adversity

Emerging research in neuroscience offers fascinating insights into how adversity can physically reshape our brains for greater resilience. When we successfully navigate challenges, our brains form new neural pathways—literally rewiring themselves to better handle future stresses. This neuroplasticity explains why exposure to manageable adversity can strengthen our capacity to handle difficulties.

Scientists at the University of California found that moderate stress actually causes stem cells in the brain to proliferate into new nerve cells, which may improve mental performance. This reinforces what many of us instinctively sense: overcoming challenges makes us mentally stronger. From a purely biological standpoint, appropriate adversity is not just character building—it's brain building.

This doesn't mean we should deliberately seek out traumatic experiences. Too much stress, especially early in life or without adequate support, can damage rather than strengthen. But it does suggest that our brains are designed to grow through challenge, not despite it.

In the next chapter, we'll explore one of the most profound teachings on finding strength in suffering by turning to a figure who epitomized resilience through pain: Jesus of Nazareth. Whether you are religious or not, Jesus's philosophy of pain—embracing suffering with love and forgiveness—offers powerful insight into how transforming pain can even change the world around us.

For now, let's end this chapter with a simple truth: Adversity is not something we wish for, but when it arrives, it can become our greatest teacher. The first step to turning pain into power is to stop seeing all pain as bad and instead see it as part of our journey, sometimes even a necessary part. Every hero's story has dark chapters, and those chapters give meaning to the hero's triumphs. The same is true for each of us. Your challenges are forging you. And that is a gift, however wrapped in thorns it may be.

Pain-to-Power Exercises – Chapter 2

1. Challenge Inventory: Make a list of three significant adversities you've faced at different points in your life (childhood, early adulthood, recent years). For each challenge, write down the following: (1) what made this difficult at the time, (2) at least one unexpected positive outcome or lesson, and (3) a specific strength you developed because of this experience. This reflection helps you recognize patterns in how you've grown through difficulty during your life, building confidence that you can transform future challenges. When facing new difficulties, revisit this inventory to remind yourself of your demonstrated capacity to grow through adversity.

2. Mindset Shift – From Problem to Teacher: The next time you experience a minor setback (a project at work goes wrong, an argument with a friend, etc.), practice reframing it on paper. Write briefly about the situation and then answer, "What can I learn from this? How might this help me improve?" Even if the only answer is, "I need to practice patience," or, "This taught me to communicate more clearly," you are extracting a lesson. This trains your brain to automatically look for growth opportunities rather than dwelling on frustration. Practice this reframing consistently for three weeks whenever you face minor setbacks to develop this mental habit.

3. Comfort Zone Stretch: Identify one area from the following areas where you've been avoiding discomfort: social (initiating a difficult conversation, attending an event alone), professional (volunteering for a presentation, asking for feedback), creative (trying a skill you might initially fail at), or physical (attempting a challenging workout). Start with something that feels mildly uncomfortable—not terrifying. Commit to one specific action this week, and then journal about what you actually did, what you learned about yourself, and how it felt to choose discomfort intentionally. This exercise builds your discomfort tolerance in a controlled way, strengthening your capacity to handle bigger challenges when they arise unexpectedly.

Having explored how adversity can strengthen us, let's turn to one of history's most profound examples of suffering transformed into redemptive power. Jesus of Nazareth's approach to pain offers universal wisdom about finding meaning in suffering that transcends any specific religious context. His example illuminates the path from sacrifice to strength that can guide our own journeys.

CHAPTER 3

Jesus and the Philosophy of Pain

Suffering, Sacrifice, and Strength – A Universal Perspective

"Father, forgive them, for they know not what they do." These words, spoken by Jesus while in excruciating pain on the cross, exemplify a profound approach to suffering. Beyond any religious context, this scene presents a powerful human truth—an innocent man in agonizing pain choosing forgiveness over fury. Jesus of Nazareth demonstrated not just bearing pain with grace, but transforming it into a force that continues to echo for billions. This chapter examines Jesus's teachings and example regarding pain, suffering, and resilience—not to preach religion, but to glean universal lessons about finding meaning and even triumph through profound adversity. His embrace of suffering, practice of forgiveness, and discovery of purpose within pain offer insights valuable to anyone seeking to transform their own struggles into strength.

The Embrace of Suffering

In Christian theology, Jesus is often called the "Man of Sorrows." He experienced hunger, homelessness, betrayal by his closest friends, public humiliation, torture, and a slow death. And yet, the narrative is that this suffering was purposeful. It was, in the Christian view, a sacrifice made out of love to redeem others. Even if one doesn't subscribe to the theology, the idea of sacrificial suffering contains a powerful lesson: enduring pain can be a source of strength when it's connected to a deeper purpose or love.

Jesus didn't seek out suffering for its own sake—when possible, he alleviated suffering (he healed the sick, fed the hungry, and consoled the sorrowful). But when faced with inevitable pain, he accepted it willingly. On the night before his crucifixion, as the story goes, Jesus prayed in the Garden of Gethsemane, overwhelmed by dread, such that his sweat fell like drops of blood. "If it be possible, let this cup pass from me," he prayed, expressing a very human desire to avoid what was coming. "Yet not my will, but thine be done." In that moment, he made a choice to embrace the pain that he believed he had to endure, out of obedience to a higher calling and love for humanity.

This deliberate acceptance of suffering for a greater purpose stands in stark contrast to our modern impulse to avoid discomfort at all costs. We live in an age of convenience, where same-day delivery, on-demand entertainment, and instant gratification are the norm. Pain—whether physical, emotional, or spiritual—is often viewed as something to eliminate immediately, not something to face with purpose. Yet in Jesus's example, we see a different approach: the willingness to move toward necessary suffering rather than away from it.

Consider how this might apply to your own life. Perhaps you've been putting off a difficult conversation because it will be uncomfortable, avoiding a needed medical procedure because of fear, or hesitating to leave a comfortable but unfulfilling job to pursue your true calling. In each case, embracing the temporary pain could lead to greater growth and fulfillment. As philosopher Kahlil Gibran wrote, "Your pain is the breaking of the shell that encloses your understanding." Sometimes, we must be willing to crack open in order to expand.

Knowing this, you can accept the pain in your life with dignity. Think of the image of Jesus carrying his own cross, which has come to symbolize a heavy burden, to the site of his execution. Symbolically, this act teaches the value of accepting one's burdens with dignity. Rather than railing against the injustice he suffered, he carried it. This isn't to say we should not resist injustice (Jesus also spoke truth to power and challenged corruption), but it highlights a key aspect of resilience: sometimes, endurance itself is a victory. Simply not giving up under extreme hardship is a triumph of the spirit.

I witnessed this kind of dignified endurance among political prisoners in Venezuela. These men and women, despite being unjustly detained and often mistreated, maintained their integrity and sense of purpose.

Forgiveness and Strength

One of the most radical aspects of Jesus's response to pain is forgiveness. Forgiving those who caused your pain can seem almost superhuman. Yet consider what forgiveness does: it breaks the cycle of pain. If Jesus on the cross had instead screamed curses at his executioners, the story would be one of understandable anger but likely perpetuated hatred. By saying, "Forgive them," he refuses to become like those who are hurting him. He holds onto his identity as a person of love and compassion, even in extreme circumstances.

Forgiveness, in a broader sense, is a powerful tool for anyone dealing with past hurt. It does not mean condoning wrongdoing or forgetting the pain. Rather, it means letting go of the hold that the wrongdoing has on your heart. It's releasing the resentment so you can heal. There's a saying: "Holding onto anger is like drinking poison and expecting the other person to die." Jesus's act of forgiving amid pain demonstrates the ultimate resilience of spirit—refusing to let bitterness destroy you. By forgiving, we take back our power from those who hurt us; we say, "You will not control my spirit."

This concept of forgiveness as liberation echoes across different traditions and disciplines. In psychology, forgiveness is increasingly recognized as crucial for mental health. Studies show that people who practice forgiveness experience lower levels of depression, anxiety, and stress, along with better cardiovascular health. The act of forgiving literally changes our bodies, reducing the harmful stress hormones that accompany long-held resentment.

I experienced this transformation firsthand when I had to forgive those who threatened my family after I fled my native land. For months, I carried a burning anger that kept me awake at night, imagining confrontations and revenge. This anger did nothing to those who had wronged me, but it poisoned my new life in America. The day I consciously chose to begin the process of forgiveness—not for their sake, but for mine—was the day I truly began to reclaim my power and peace.

In practical terms, if someone has caused you deep pain, forgiving them might be one of the hardest things you ever do. It may also be one of the most liberating. It's a process that can take time and doesn't necessarily involve reconciling or forgetting. But it lightens the emotional load you carry, in turn making you stronger and more free to move forward.

Finding Meaning and Purpose in Suffering

Jesus's suffering is depicted as having cosmic meaning—redeeming humanity. Most of us won't have such world-altering interpretations of our pain. However, we can find personal meaning in our suffering, which is a concept psychiatrist Viktor Frankl (whom we'll discuss in the next chapter) also emphasized. For Jesus, the crucifixion was followed by resurrection. In our own lives, suffering can lead to some form of rebirth or renewal. Often, people describe a "new self" that emerges after a period of pain, almost as if the old self "dies" during the struggle and a new self comes to life. This map of pain->death->rebirth is a powerful pattern seen in myths and stories across cultures. (The hero's journey often involves a metaphorical death and rebirth.) Jesus's story is one archetypal example.

This pattern of transformation through suffering appears in countless human experiences. Consider the parent who loses a child and eventually channels that grief into founding a charity that helps other children; the recovering addict who, having walked through the "valley of the shadow of death," emerges with wisdom and compassion that they use to guide others toward sobriety; or the cancer survivor whose brush with mortality awakens them to a deeper appreciation of life and a commitment to living authentically.

In my own journey, leaving Venezuela—my home, my culture, my identity—felt like a kind of death. I mourned the life I had known and the future I had imagined there. But through that painful transition, a new version of me emerged: more adaptable, more compassionate toward other immigrants, and more aware of what truly matters. The suffering became purposeful because it reshaped me into someone capable of helping others navigate similar challenges.

Another teaching of Jesus relevant here is the idea of taking up your cross daily. This suggests that enduring life's challenges with faith and perseverance is a daily practice, not a one-time event. It implies commitment to a purpose despite ongoing difficulties. Whether one's purpose is raising children, serving the community, excelling in an art or profession, or a spiritual quest, keeping that purpose front and center can make heavy burdens more bearable. The "cross" you carry gains meaning when it's connected to love or principle.

We should also mention that Jesus showed vulnerability in suffering. On the cross, he cried out, "My God, my God, why have you forsaken me?"—a moment of deep anguish and even doubt. This is important: even someone seen as supremely holy had moments of despair. Feeling doubt or hopelessness in your pain does not mean you are failing at resilience. It means you're human. What matters is that, like Jesus, you don't let that moment of agony be your final moment. He still, at the end, entrusted his spirit and expressed love. Likewise, we can acknowledge when we feel abandoned or broken and still choose, in the end, to hope or to love again. Resilience doesn't mean never crying out in pain; it means continuing on after you cry out.

This permission to be fully human in our suffering—to acknowledge our pain and doubt—is perhaps one of the most comforting aspects of Jesus's example. Too often, especially in some spiritual circles, there's pressure to maintain a facade of unshakable faith or constant positivity. Jesus's cry of abandonment tears through that pretense and creates space for authentic struggle. When we allow ourselves to acknowledge our darkest moments, we often find that we're not alone in them.

Universal Lessons Beyond Christianity

While we have focused on Jesus, these lessons resonate beyond any one religion. Many spiritual traditions uphold similar ideals: finding purpose in pain, responding to suffering with compassion, and emerging stronger.

In Buddhism, suffering (*dukkha*) is acknowledged as a fundamental aspect of existence, but also as a doorway to enlightenment. The Buddha himself went through extreme asceticism (self-denial) and nearly died before finding the Middle Way. Buddhist teachings emphasize that our relationship to suffering—rather than the suffering itself—determines much of our experience. The concept of compassion (*karuna*) in Buddhism parallels Jesus's emphasis on love; both traditions suggest that opening our hearts to others, even in our own pain, can channel suffering into meaningful connection.

A beautiful illustration of this comes from the story of Kisa Gotami, a woman who sought the Buddha's help when her child died. Consumed by grief, she carried her dead son from house to house, begging for medicine to revive him. The Buddha asked her to bring him a mustard seed from a house where no one had ever died. As she searched, she gradually realized that death and suffering touch every home. This awakening to the universality of suffering became the beginning of her healing and eventual enlightenment. Like Jesus's transformation of suffering into redemption, Kisa's grief became the pathway to profound wisdom.

In Hinduism, the concepts of karma (an action, work, or deed and its effect or consequences) and dharma (duty) may lead one to accept suffering as part of one's righteous path or duty. The Bhagavad Gita tells of Arjuna, a warrior torn by the prospect of fighting his own kinsmen. Krishna counsels him to fulfill his duty (dharma) with detachment from the outcome, teaching that enduring the suffering of difficult choices is sometimes necessary for spiritual growth. The Hindu saint Ramakrishna taught that spiritual seekers should "welcome suffering, for it hastens the destruction of the ego."

In Islam, enduring trials with patience (*sabr*) is a highly praised virtue, with the belief that God knows the weight of your struggles and will reward perseverance.

32

The Quran states, "And We will surely test you with something of fear and hunger and a loss of wealth and lives and fruits, but give good tidings to the patient" (2:155). The Prophet Muhammad endured persecution, exile, poverty, and the death of his children with steadfast faith, modeling how to maintain dignity and purpose through suffering.

In secular terms, we can think of figures like Martin Luther King Jr. or Mahatma Gandhi, who, inspired by Jesus, among others, practiced non-violence and met suffering with dignity and love—and in doing so, changed societies. King, facing jail and threats, said that unearned suffering is redemptive; he meant that willingly absorbing violence without retaliating can transform the oppressor and awaken the conscience of a nation. That is exactly what happened in the American Civil Rights Movement.

What emerges from examining these diverse traditions—from Buddhism's mindful acceptance of suffering and Islam's emphasis on patient endurance to Hinduism's concepts of duty to secular movements for social change—is that the transformative approach to suffering transcends any single religious or cultural framework. These convergent wisdoms suggest that facing pain with purpose and dignity represents a universal human insight rather than merely a particular theological position.

Gandhi's concept of *satyagraha* (truth-force or soul-force) similarly embraced suffering as a means of moral transformation. When asked about his strategy, Gandhi explained that the goal was not to defeat the opponent but to transform them through voluntary suffering. "The idea is to suffer in your own person," he said, "so as to bring home to the wrongdoer the injustice of his action." This philosophy led to India's independence and inspired non-violent movements worldwide.

The philosophy of pain that Jesus exemplifies is about transforming the energy of suffering into the energy of love. It's alchemy of the spirit: hatred and pain in, forgiveness and compassion out. When we manage to do this even in small ways in our own lives, we experience a sort of triumph that is spiritual or moral. It's a quiet triumph, unseen by the world perhaps, but deeply powerful. It's responding to a hurtful coworker with patience instead of anger, or choosing to volunteer and help others even while you yourself are grieving, or simply not letting a chronic pain condition steal your gratitude for life.

The Power of Community in Suffering

One more universal takeaway from Jesus's approach to suffering is the idea of community and support. In his hardest hours, Jesus was not completely alone—he had friends (even though some fell asleep or denied him, a few stayed), and according to the accounts, even on the cross he spoke to a friend and made sure his mother would be cared for. He also expressed feeling forsaken, which indicates how important the presence of support is. For us, this underlines the importance of not suffering in silence if you can help it. Seek out friends, family, support groups, or spiritual counsel. Let others help carry your cross at times. Even the strongest figures benefit from compassion and help. (Simon of Cyrene helped Jesus carry the cross part of the way in the story.) Leaning on others is not a weakness; it can be life-saving and can transform pain into bonding.

This communal aspect of enduring suffering appears across cultures. In many African traditions, for instance, the concept of Ubuntu ("I am because we are") emphasizes that our humanity is inextricably bound up with others. When one person suffers, the community shares the burden. In Japanese culture, the concept of *amae* describes the comforting dependence on another person—recognizing that interdependence, not rugged individualism, often carries us through our darkest times.

Modern research confirms what these traditions have long known: social connection is one of the strongest predictors of resilience in the face of trauma. Studies of Holocaust survivors, combat veterans, and natural disaster victims consistently show that those with strong social bonds fare better psychologically than those who face adversity alone. As researcher Dr. Bessel van der Kolk puts it, "Being able to feel safe with other people is probably the single most important aspect of mental health."

I experienced this truth when I first arrived in the United States. Despite priding myself on independence and strength, I found myself overwhelmed by the challenges of building a new life in a foreign culture. It was only when I connected with a community of fellow immigrants—people who understood my journey without explanation—that I began to truly heal. We shared meals, stories, and practical advice. More importantly, we shared our vulnerability. As in the story of Jesus, where disciples gathered at the foot of the cross, there is profound power in simply being present with one another in suffering.

Practical Application: Living the Philosophy

How might we practically apply Jesus's philosophy of pain in our everyday lives? Consider these approaches:

1. **Practice purposeful acceptance:** When facing unavoidable suffering, ask yourself, "What purpose might this serve? What values am I honoring by enduring this?" This doesn't mean you pretend the pain isn't real—it means you frame it within a meaningful context.

2. **Choose forgiveness as a path to freedom:** Remember that forgiveness is primarily for your benefit, not the offender's. Start small with forgiving minor grudges before tackling deeper hurts. Notice how the act of forgiving—even silently, even partially—creates space for healing.

3. **Embrace vulnerability:** Allow yourself to acknowledge when you're struggling, both to yourself and to trusted others. Jesus's cry of abandonment reminds us that even in spiritual traditions, authentic expression of pain is honored.

4. **Find community in suffering:** Resist the temptation to isolate when in pain. Seek out others who understand your struggle, whether through support groups, faith communities, or close relationships. Both receiving and offering support create meaning in difficult times.

5. **Look for resurrection possibilities:** After significant suffering, consciously ask, "How might I be reborn through this experience? What

35

new understanding or strength might emerge?" Sometimes, writing your pain story with an eye toward transformation can reveal patterns of growth you hadn't noticed.

In summary, Jesus's teachings and life show that suffering can contain meaning, love is stronger than pain, and the way we choose to bear our sorrows can inspire and uplift others. Whether one views him as divine or as an archetype of the suffering hero, the lessons are powerful. We learn that pain need not destroy our humanity and can instead elevate it.

Just as Jesus found purpose through pain, other spiritual figures and traditions have echoed this wisdom throughout history. The Buddha's journey through suffering to enlightenment, Gandhi's willing embrace of hardship for social change, and countless ordinary people who have transformed personal tragedy into service. All demonstrate that pain, when approached with purpose and compassion, can become a catalyst for profound growth.

Pain-to-Power Exercises – Chapter 3

1. Reflection on Forgiveness: Think of someone who hurt you in the past (it could be mild or severe). Write a private letter to them (you don't have to send it) expressing how you felt because of their actions. Acknowledge the pain. Then, in the letter, write the words, "I forgive you." Observe how it feels to write that. Does it bring up resistance, sadness, or relief? Forgiveness is often a process, not a one-time switch. This exercise is just a start. Consider what forgiving this person would mean for you (regardless of whether they deserve it or not). You're not excusing what happened; you are choosing to let go of the burden of anger. Even if you're not ready to fully forgive, notice any small shift in how tightly you hold the pain.

2. Carrying Your Cross – Identify Purpose: Identify a hardship you are currently facing. Now ask yourself: "What larger purpose or value can I connect this to?" For example, "I am going through painful physical therapy, but I endure it so I can regain mobility to play with my kids," or, "I feel lonely after moving to a new city, but I endure it because I value my career opportunity here, and I'm building a better future." Write down the purpose that gives meaning to your suffering. Whenever the pain feels pointless, revisit what you wrote to remind yourself why you carry this cross. This exercise helps transform seemingly meaningless suffering into purposeful endurance by connecting it to your deeper values.

3. Support System Check-In: Jesus had help and companionship on his journey of suffering. Who are the people or communities that support you in tough times? Make a list of your "support system" (friends, family, mentors, support groups, faith community, etc.). If you realize this list is short, think about ways to expand it—perhaps by reaching out to old friends, joining a class or support group, or talking to a counselor or faith leader. If the list is robust, consider reaching out to one person on it and simply thanking them or checking in. Often, knowing we're not alone in our pain can give us strength. This exercise reminds you that resilience flourishes in connection rather than isolation.

Jesus showed us one powerful approach to finding purpose in pain. Now let's broaden our exploration to examine how various wisdom traditions and modern psychology understand the relationship between suffering and meaning. Viktor Frankl, Buddhist teachings, and existential philosophy offer complementary perspectives that deepen our understanding of how meaning transforms our relationship with pain.

CHAPTER 4

Meaning in Suffering

Finding Purpose in the Pain – Frankl, Buddhism, and Existential Wisdom

During World War II, amid the darkest depths of a Nazi concentration camp, Viktor Frankl observed something remarkable: those who found meaning in their suffering were more likely to survive. As a psychiatrist who lost his wife, parents, and friends to the Holocaust, Frankl forged a profound truth about resilience through his own unimaginable suffering. "If there is meaning in life at all," he wrote, "then there must be meaning in suffering." This chapter explores how we can find purpose within our pain, drawing on Frankl's insights, Buddhist teachings, and existential philosophy. When suffering is unavoidable, meaning becomes the lifeline that carries us through.

Viktor Frankl and the Will to Meaning

Viktor Frankl's experience and psychology offer perhaps the clearest framework for transforming suffering into meaning. He called his approach *logotherapy*, from *logos*, the Greek word for "meaning" or "purpose." Frankl believed that the primary drive in humans is not pleasure (as Freud thought) or power (as Adler thought), but meaning. We crave a sense of purpose for our lives. Suffering, in this view, can be endurable if it has a reason. But take away meaning, and even comfort can feel empty. One of Frankl's most powerful insights: "In some ways suffering ceases to be suffering at the moment it finds a meaning."

Let me share a story that illustrates this principle. During my early days in the United States, I worked a physically demanding job stocking shelves at a home improvement store. The work was grueling—heavy lifting for hours in changing temperatures, often starting at 4:00 a.m. My body ached constantly, and sometimes, in moments of exhaustion, I questioned whether I had made the right choice in leaving Venezuela.

What transformed this suffering was attaching meaning to it. Each box I lifted, each shelf I stocked was not just physical labor; it was providing for my family, funding my education to rebuild my career, and establishing our new life in a country where we could be free. The work itself didn't change, but my relationship to it did. The pain in my muscles became a reminder of my purpose rather than just meaningless suffering.

How does one find meaning in suffering? In the concentration camp, Frankl found meaning by imagining himself in the future giving lectures about the psychology of the camps, helping others find hope. He found meaning in tending to fellow prisoners, observing moments of beauty (like a sunset) even in misery, and holding on to the love he had for his wife (not knowing if she was alive or dead). Those sources of meaning kept his spirit alive. Many others succumbed to what he called "give-up-itis"—a despair that led them to lose the will to live. The difference often came down to whether they could see their suffering as serving some purpose beyond mere torture.

Frankl identified three primary sources of meaning that humans can access, even in dire situations:

1. **Purpose through creative work or deeds** - contributing something valuable to the world.

2. **Purpose through experiences and encounters** - loving others and appreciating beauty.

3. **Purpose through the attitude we take toward unavoidable suffering** - finding dignity in how we face challenges.

This third source is especially relevant when discussing pain and adversity. Even when we cannot change our circumstances, we can always choose our stance toward them. In Frankl's own words: "Everything can be taken from a man but one thing: the last of the human freedoms—to choose one's attitude in any given set of circumstances, to choose one's own way."

In a much-quoted passage, Frankl recalled a fellow prisoner who was contemplating suicide because he felt he had nothing left to live for. Frankl helped him realize that life was still expecting something from him—in this case, a child abroad who was alive and waiting, and research papers he had written that needed to be finished. In recognizing that his life still had a purpose, he found the strength to endure a bit longer.

Frankl's approach for us is this: when you are in pain, ask what or who is still expecting something from you. What task remains for you? What love calls to you? It could be your family, your art, your faith, or your community—anything that gives a larger significance to your individual suffering.

It's important to note that finding meaning is very personal. No one else can impose meaning on your suffering. ("Everything happens for a reason," can sometimes be a hurtful cliché if said dismissively by others.) The meaning must come from within, from your own values and perspective. And sometimes, you might not find meaning until after the fact. It's hard to find meaning in a fresh wound. But as time heals, you may see how that wound changed your life's direction in a meaningful way.

The Buddhist Perspective: Pain as an Opportunity for Enlightenment

Buddhism squarely addresses suffering (*dukkha*) as a fundamental truth of life. Far from seeing suffering as merely negative, Buddhism treats it as the starting point for wisdom. The Buddha taught that by examining our suffering, we can understand its causes—chiefly craving and attachment—and by understanding, we can alleviate suffering.

One teaching relevant here is the two arrows analogy. The Buddha said that when struck by a painful event, an untrained person shoots a second arrow into themselves by reacting with aversion: "Why me? This is awful!" The initial pain is the first arrow (often inevitable in life). The second arrow is the additional suffering we heap on through mental reactions like anger, resistance, or catastrophizing. The practice of mindfulness helps us stop that second arrow. We learn to experience pain with acceptance rather than magnifying it with panic or bitterness.

To make this concrete, imagine you receive news that you've been passed over for a promotion at work. The first arrow is the disappointment and genuine sadness—these are natural, unavoidable reactions. The second arrow comes when you start thinking, "This always happens to me. I'll never succeed. My boss hates me. My career is over." Those thoughts create additional suffering beyond the initial disappointment. Buddhism teaches us to recognize when we're shooting that second arrow and to practice letting those thoughts go.

But beyond reducing extra suffering, Buddhism offers the idea that suffering can lead to compassion. A Buddhist practitioner uses their own pain as a way to cultivate empathy for others. For instance, if I am suffering from heartbreak, I can reflect, "Countless others have felt this same pain of loss. May I use this experience to understand and help others who suffer?" This transforms personal pain into a source of connection with humanity—a deeply meaningful approach.

Some Buddhist meditations (like Tonglen in Tibetan practice) even involve breathing in the suffering of others and breathing out relief or love to them, using one's own painful experiences as a bridge to feeling what others feel. In doing so, pain becomes a vehicle for developing compassion and loving-kindness, which are considered high achievements on the path to enlightenment.

Buddhist philosophy also emphasizes impermanence: "This too shall pass." Knowing that pain is not permanent can itself be meaningful, as it reminds us that all experiences are transient. Even if a pain lasts a lifetime, our relationship to it can change. Many who suffer chronic pain or disability find meaning in how they come to accept and live with their condition, often inspiring others by example.

Finally, Buddhism (and Hinduism as well) introduces the concept of karma—the idea that our actions have consequences that shape our future experiences. Some interpret this to mean if you suffer now, perhaps it balances something or teaches something for the future (though one must be careful; it's not about blaming victims for their suffering, but encouraging the individual to respond skillfully to whatever happens). The actionable part of karma is that you can always choose your next action, and that is your path out of suffering. As the Dalai Lama has said, compassion and ethical living are the surest ways to a happier life, even amidst pain.

Existential Philosophy: Creating Your Own Meaning

Beyond Frankl and Buddhism, existential philosophers like Friedrich Nietzsche and Jean-Paul Sartre have wrestled with suffering's role. Nietzsche famously said, "To live is to suffer, to survive is to find some meaning in the suffering." He himself endured great physical pain and illness throughout life, yet his philosophy praised the idea of the "Übermensch"—one who could affirm life, suffering and all, and turn it into art or achievement.

To understand Nietzsche's approach, imagine an artist who incorporates a paint spill (an accident, a "suffering" in the creative process) into the artwork, making it an intentional element of the final piece. The artist doesn't pretend the spill didn't happen; they transform it into something meaningful. Similarly, Nietzsche suggests we incorporate our hardships into our life's "artwork," making them essential rather than regrettable elements of who we are becoming.

In one of his more poetic images, Nietzsche suggested one should say yes to life, in even its strangest and hardest aspects, as if willing them to recur eternally (his concept of eternal recurrence). It's an attitude of embracing the full experience of existence, suffering included, and even loving it because it's yours and it makes you who you are. This is sometimes summarized in the Latin phrase *amor fati*—"love of fate." Loving your fate doesn't mean you have to enjoy pain, but that you accept it as your story and see it as an integral piece of your life's artwork.

Jean-Paul Sartre and Albert Camus, twentieth-century existentialists, considered a universe that might inherently have no meaning (if one does not believe in a divine plan). In such a case, they argued, humans must create meaning. Camus, in his famous essay *The Myth of Sisyphus*, imagines Sisyphus, condemned by the gods to roll a boulder up a hill for eternity only to have it roll back down each time. It is pointless, absurd suffering, yet Camus concludes, "One must imagine Sisyphus happy." Why? Because Camus suggests that Sisyphus can own his fate; by choosing to push the boulder and not despair, he defies the absurdity. In a sense, rebellion against meaningless suffering itself creates a kind of meaning. Camus implies that the act of living and finding joy despite the absurd is a heroic and defining human stance.

To make this more relatable, consider someone diagnosed with a chronic illness that has no cure. The situation might seem absurd and unfair—a boulder that must be pushed uphill daily with no final victory possible. The existentialist perspective would say that choosing to live well despite this condition, finding moments of joy and purpose while acknowledging the struggle, is itself a profound act of meaning-making. The meaning isn't in the illness; it's in the response to it.

For us, in practical terms, existentialism says: even if your suffering seems meaningless at first, you have the power to give it meaning through your choices. Maybe there's no grand cosmic reason that you lost your job or got sick—that might just be random. But you can choose a response that gives it purpose: perhaps you pivot to a new career that fulfills you more or become an advocate for others with your illness. The event itself might not be inherently meaningful, but your response can fill it with meaning.

Post-Traumatic Growth: Scientific Evidence for Meaning Through Suffering

While philosophical and spiritual traditions have long recognized the potential for growth through suffering, modern psychology has now documented this phenomenon scientifically. Researchers Richard Tedeschi and Lawrence Calhoun coined the term "post-traumatic growth" to describe the positive psychological changes that can emerge from the struggle with highly challenging life circumstances.

Studies have found that many people who face severe adversity report profound positive changes in five main areas:

1. **Greater appreciation of life and changed priorities:** After trauma, people often report valuing simple everyday pleasures more deeply and prioritizing meaningful relationships over material success.

2. **Warmer, more intimate relationships**: Having faced their own vulnerability, many people develop deeper connections with others and become more comfortable with emotional intimacy.

3. **Greater sense of personal strength**: Surviving difficulty can reveal inner resources people didn't know they had, leading to statements like "If I survived that, I can handle anything."

4. **Recognition of new possibilities or paths in life**: Trauma often forces people to reconsider their life direction, sometimes opening doors to unexpected new pursuits or passions.

5. **Spiritual development**: Many people report deeper spiritual understanding or connection after facing extreme challenges, regardless of their specific religious beliefs.

This research doesn't suggest that trauma is "good" or that suffering should be sought out. Rather, it confirms what wisdom traditions have long taught: humans have a remarkable capacity to extract meaning and growth from painful experiences.

When I speak with fellow Venezuelan immigrants who have rebuilt their lives in new countries, I'm struck by how many describe this pattern of growth. Despite the pain of leaving their homeland, many say they've discovered strengths they never knew they had, developed a deeper appreciation for family bonds, found new career paths they might never have explored otherwise, and gained perspective on what truly matters in life.

The Stories We Tell Ourselves

At the core of finding meaning in suffering is the story we tell about it. Humans are storytellers. We constantly narrate our lives in our minds, interpreting events and weaving them into a personal narrative. When something painful happens, that narrative often splinters: "This isn't how it was supposed to go." To heal, we often need to rewrite our narrative, including the pain as an important chapter, not the end of the book.

For example, someone who goes through a traumatic accident might initially think, *My life is ruined. I'll never be the same, and nothing good can come of this.* That's an understandable initial story. Finding meaning might involve slowly editing that story to: "The accident was a terrible turning point. It limited me in some ways, but it opened my eyes in others. It taught me to value life and inspired me to help others in similar situations. It's not what I wanted, but it gave my life a new direction." That revised story doesn't deny the tragedy; it places it in a context where the protagonist (you) finds something to live for through it.

I witnessed this narrative transformation in a close friend who was wrongfully imprisoned during Venezuela's political turmoil. In the first months after his release, his story was one of bitterness and loss—focused on the injustice, the stolen years, and the opportunities missed. Over time, though, his narrative evolved. Without minimizing the wrong done to him, he began to incorporate how the experience had clarified his values, deepened his appreciation for freedom, and given him a powerful platform to advocate for others still imprisoned. The pain didn't disappear from his story, but it became part of a larger narrative of purpose and resilience.

Therapists often use techniques of narrative therapy or cognitive reframing to assist people in this process. One exercise is writing a "resilience narrative"—basically, writing about your suffering from the perspective of a hero's journey, where you are the hero overcoming trials. It may feel odd, but it highlights that how we frame an experience matters. Are you the victim of your story or the hero? The facts might be the same, but the angle differs. By choosing the hero's stance, you imbue your suffering with dignity and purpose.

A Caution: When Meaning is Elusive

It's worth noting that not every pain is immediately redeemable by meaning, and that's okay. Some suffering is so senseless and cruel (like the loss of a child, or violence and abuse) that telling someone to "find meaning" can sound offensive. Meaning in suffering is often something that we discover for ourselves over time, not something anyone else can prescribe. If you are in the raw throes of grief or trauma, you might not be ready to ponder meaning yet—and you shouldn't feel pressured to. Sometimes the only "meaning" to cling to is that staying alive and putting one foot in front of the other will eventually lead you to new experiences where meaning can grow again.

This is particularly important to emphasize: meaning-making is not a replacement for proper care and support during times of suffering. If you're experiencing depression, trauma, or overwhelming grief, professional help may be necessary. Finding meaning is not about denying or minimizing pain; it's about eventually integrating that pain into a life that still has purpose.

In the immediate aftermath of tragedy, survival and self-care are enough. But as wounds scar over, meaning often gently emerges. Many bereaved parents, for example, eventually start foundations or campaigns in their child's memory, turning their agony into a force for good so that their child's life, however short, radiates impact. Many survivors of injustice become activists, ensuring that their pain was "not in vain" by preventing others from suffering similarly. These are profound ways meaning can arise from pain.

Sometimes, meaning can simply be in endurance: the sheer act of continuing forward represents a triumph of the human spirit. In situations where no larger purpose seems evident, the commitment to persevere—to witness another day, to maintain dignity amid suffering, to refuse to be destroyed by pain—becomes itself a profound meaning. As Holocaust survivor and author Elie Wiesel suggested, sometimes bearing witness, simply enduring so that the story can be told, is meaning enough.

The Role of Community in Meaning-Making

While meaning-making is deeply personal, it rarely happens in isolation. Communities play a crucial role in helping us find purpose in our pain. When suffering isolates us, connection with others who understand can help us reframe our experience.

Support groups for people facing similar challenges—whether grief, addiction, illness, or trauma—provide not just emotional comfort but also models for finding meaning. Seeing how others have integrated their suffering into a purposeful life gives us templates for our own journey. When a cancer survivor mentors a newly diagnosed patient, or when parents who have lost children come together to support each other, the meaning they create is both individual and collective.

This communal aspect of meaning-making appears in many spiritual traditions. In Jewish communities, the practice of sitting shiva after a death involves the community gathering around the bereaved, acknowledging their pain, and helping them begin to make sense of their loss. In many indigenous cultures, healing rituals after trauma involve the whole community witnessing and validating both the suffering and the path forward.

Even in secular contexts, sharing our pain stories with trusted others who can listen without judgment or easy answers helps us begin to articulate meaning. Sometimes we discover what our suffering means to us only when we try to explain it to someone else.

In conclusion, finding meaning in suffering is a deeply personal but powerful strategy in turning pain into strength. Whether through Frankl's lens of purpose, Buddhism's lens of compassion and insight, or existentialism's lens of chosen purpose, the common thread is that our minds can extract value from even the harshest experiences. This meaning doesn't erase pain, but it can make pain useful—fuel for growth, connection, art, service, or personal evolution.

As you reflect on your own life, you might identify a painful event and ask, How did I change after that? What did I learn? What meaning did it add to my life story? If the answers aren't clear yet, that's fine. They may reveal themselves in time.

Next, we will turn to the science of resilience to further understand how people cope and rebound after adversity, complementing this search for meaning with research on the biological and psychological mechanisms that help us survive and thrive after trauma.

Pain-to-Power Exercises — Chapter 4

1. Create a "Meaning Map": Take a piece of paper and draw three columns. In the first column, list two to three difficult experiences you have had. In the second column, write what you felt or feel the purpose of each experience could be (even if it's hard to see, make a guess like "Maybe it taught me X" or "It brought me to Y place/person" or "It changed my perspective on Z"). In the third column, note how you have changed or grown from it. This exercise helps you explicitly connect pain to meaning and growth. If some experiences still feel meaningless, leave them or write "TBD"—that's okay. Revisiting this map later might show new meanings emerging as you grow.

2. Mantra of Purpose: Think of a short phrase that encapsulates the meaning you want to assign to your current struggle. For example: "This pain will make me stronger," or "I am using this suffering to deepen my compassion," or "I will create something good out of this." It should feel authentic and motivating to you. Repeat this phrase to yourself each morning or when the pain feels heavy. Over time, this reaffirms a purposeful narrative in your mind. This practice, inspired by Viktor Frankl's approach, helps you develop a meaning-oriented perspective that transforms how you experience difficult situations.

3. Service from Suffering: One way to find meaning is to turn your pain into service. Identify one small way you can use what you've been through to help someone else. If you lost someone, maybe you can reach out in support to a friend who's lost someone. If you went through illness, you might share a tip that helped you with another patient. If you suffered discrimination, you might mentor someone from your community. It could even be as simple as writing a blog post about your experience and how you coped. Doing this not only helps others but also transforms your pain into an act of empathy and solidarity—a deeply meaningful outcome.

Having explored how finding meaning transforms our relationship with suffering, let's now turn to the science behind our capacity for resilience. While previous chapters examined philosophical and spiritual approaches to pain, **Chapter 5** will illuminate what modern research reveals about the biological and psychological foundations of human resilience.

By understanding the brain's remarkable ability to adapt after trauma, the psychological factors that promote recovery, and the social connections that sustain us through difficulty, we gain a comprehensive picture of how humans not only survive adversity but often grow stronger because of it. This scientific understanding complements the meaning-making approaches we've explored, showing how our innate capacity for resilience operates at the neurological, psychological, and social levels.

CHAPTER 5

The Science of Resilience

How We Overcome: The Brain, The Mind, and The Factors of Fortitude

Why do some people transform hardship into growth while others crumble under relatively minor setbacks? What happens in our brains and minds as we develop the capacity to bounce back from adversity? This chapter pivots from philosophy to science, revealing the biological and psychological foundations of resilience. Research in psychology and neuroscience offers fascinating insights into how we physically and mentally overcome challenges. Most encouragingly, resilience isn't fixed at birth—it's a set of skills and capacities we can develop throughout life. We'll explore key mechanisms that support resilience: brain plasticity that allows for new neural pathways after trauma, mindset shifts that transform our relationship with difficulty, and the inner and outer resources that fuel our ability to withstand and grow through adversity.

What is Resilience?

Psychologists define resilience in various ways, but a simple definition is the ability to recover from or adjust to misfortune or change. Imagine resilience as a rubber band's elasticity—you stretch it with stress, and it returns to its shape. Some people even thrive (grow stronger) after stress, not just returning to baseline; this is post-traumatic growth, as we discussed. Resilience isn't about never feeling pain or distress; it's about being able to endure and continue on, perhaps even with more wisdom, after the storm has passed.

I witnessed resilience firsthand in my homeland of Venezuela, particularly during the severe economic crisis when monthly inflation reached over 1,000,000 percent in 2018. I saw neighbors who had lost everything—their savings rendered worthless, their businesses shuttered—somehow find the strength to reinvent themselves. One woman I knew, a former accountant, began selling homemade empanadas from her apartment window when her office closed. Within months, she had developed a thriving microbusiness that supported her family. She hadn't just survived; she had adapted and found a new path forward. That is resilience in action—not the absence of suffering, but the presence of adaptability and perseverance.

Research has identified certain protective factors that make resilience more likely. Emmy Werner's famous Kauai longitudinal study followed a group of children born into poverty and risk factors. She found roughly one-third of them thrived in adulthood despite high adversities. Those resilient children tended to have things in common: a supportive relationship with at least one adult, an outgoing or problem-solving personality, and a skill or hobby that gave them pride. In short, connection, confidence, and coping skills protected them. This suggests resilience is part individual (traits and skills) and part environmental (support systems, community).

The Brain's Resilience: Neuroplasticity and Stress

Neuroscience has shed light on how the brain deals with stress and trauma. Our brains have an amazing property called neuroplasticity—the ability to rewire and change throughout life. When we undergo a tough experience, our brain circuits and chemistry adjust. For instance, chronic stress might oversensitize the amygdala (the fear center) and weaken the prefrontal cortex (the rational part that regulates emotions), leading to anxiety or impulsivity. However, with recovery time or training (like therapy or meditation), the brain can form new circuits that calm the amygdala and strengthen control. This is literal resilience in the brain: after trauma, some people's brains adapt to become calmer and more focused than before. Practices like mindfulness have been shown on brain scans to increase connections in areas associated with emotional regulation and decrease reactivity in stress circuits.

To make this more concrete, consider what happens when we learn to ride a bicycle. At first, it's stressful—we wobble, we fall, we might even get hurt. But with practice, our brains literally build new neural pathways. Eventually, riding becomes effortless, even enjoyable. The same process happens when we face life challenges. Initially, a setback like losing a job might trigger intense stress and anxiety. But as we work through it—updating our resume, networking, learning new skills—our brains build pathways for handling this type of stress. If we face job insecurity again in the future, those neural pathways are already there, making our response more measured and effective.

One fascinating line of research on resilience comes from studies of people who have experienced extreme stress, like prisoners of war or Special Forces training, and why some develop PTSD while others don't. There's evidence that optimism and a sense of control can biologically dampen the stress response. If your brain perceives that you have some control over a stressor, it will produce less of the stress hormone cortisol, for example. This is why reframing a situation as a challenge you can meet (rather than an overwhelming threat) actually changes what happens in your body—lower heart rate, clearer thinking. It's the difference between panic and courage at the physiological level.

Research at Harvard Medical School found that Navy SEALs in training actually showed different physiological responses to stress compared to recruits who dropped out. The successful trainees had a faster return to baseline heart rate and lower stress hormones after intense challenges. Interestingly, this wasn't just innate—through repeated exposure to controlled stress during training, their bodies literally learned to recover more efficiently. This suggests that we can train our physiological stress response through gradual exposure to challenges, much like building physical endurance through consistent exercise.

There's also research into the genetics of resilience. Some gene variants make individuals more stress-resistant (for instance, genes affecting serotonin or neuropeptide Y). But genes are not destiny; they interact with the environment. A person with "risk" genes for depression might do fine in a nurturing environment, whereas a person with "protective" genes could still struggle if exposed to relentless trauma. Still, knowing that some brains have a head start in resilience reminds us that if you struggle more with stress, it's not because you're "weak"—you may just have to work more actively to build resilience, much like someone not naturally athletic might train harder to run a marathon. And it can be done.

The emerging field of epigenetics has further revealed that our experiences can actually change how our genes express themselves, without altering the genetic code itself. Studies show that practices like meditation, exercise, and positive social connections can turn on genes associated with health and resilience while turning off genes linked to inflammation and stress. This means that even if you weren't born with the most optimal genetic profile for resilience, your daily habits and choices can significantly influence how your genes function.

One remarkable study showed that most people, even after severe trauma, do eventually recover to a baseline of mental health. In fact, reports of growth and resilience are far more common than chronic dysfunction. Our brains and bodies evolved to handle stress—to a point. The key is giving ourselves the right support and mindset to encourage those natural healing processes.

Psychology of Resilience: Mindset and Attitude

Perhaps the most important psychological factor in resilience is one we encountered in previous chapters: meaning or mindset. Pioneering psychologist Martin Seligman found that optimism correlates with resilience. Optimism here doesn't mean blind cheerfulness, but a belief that setbacks are temporary and surmountable, and that they are not one's personal failure but often due to external or specific factors. This optimistic explanatory style can be learned. For example, someone fails a test. A pessimistic thought: *I'm stupid; I'll never succeed* (personal, permanent). An optimistic reframing: *I was tired, and the test was hard—I can study differently and do better next time* (specific, temporary). Teaching people to challenge catastrophic thoughts and replace them with realistic optimism is a cornerstone of cognitive-behavioral therapy (CBT), which has a strong track record in building resilience against depression and anxiety.

Seligman's research with insurance sales agents provides a striking example of this principle in action. He found that optimistic salespeople sold 37 percent more insurance than pessimistic ones and were half as likely to quit during their first year. When faced with inevitable rejection (a common experience in sales), optimistic individuals interpreted it as a temporary setback or a challenge to improve their technique, while pessimistic individuals were more likely to see it as evidence of personal inadequacy. The difference wasn't in how many rejections they faced, but in how they interpreted and responded to those rejections.

Another powerful concept is the "growth mindset" studied by Carol Dweck. This is the belief that abilities and traits are not fixed but can be developed. If you have a growth mindset, a failure doesn't define you; it's seen as a problem to solve or a skill to improve. Applied to emotional resilience, one might think, *I'm not good at handling criticism yet, but I can get better* instead of *I just can't handle any criticism.* A growth mindset makes you more likely to persevere through challenges because you see yourself as a work in progress.

In my own journey, this growth mindset proved transformative when I faced the daunting challenge of mastering English as an adult immigrant. Each mistake in pronunciation or grammar initially felt like evidence that I would never truly belong in my new country. But gradually, I shifted to viewing these errors as valuable data points—each correction was teaching me something new. This perspective transformed language learning from a source of shame to an opportunity for growth. Within two years, I was comfortable enough to begin teaching others, not because I had become perfect, but because I had embraced the process of continuous improvement.

Self-efficacy is another factor—basically your confidence that you can do what needs to be done. The psychologist Albert Bandura showed that people who have a strong sense of self-efficacy approach challenges as something to be mastered rather than avoided. Past successes build future confidence, which is why it's important to celebrate even small victories when recovering from adversity. Each day you get out of bed and face the world while depressed, for instance, is a victory that proves you can do hard things. Taking stock of those wins builds your resilient identity: "I am someone who can overcome."

Emotion regulation skills contribute to resilience as well. Being able to soothe oneself under stress (through breathing techniques, positive self-talk, or other coping methods) can prevent a downward spiral. This is part of what separates someone who gets upset but calms down and strategizes versus someone who gets upset and then has a panic attack or rage episode that worsens the situation. The great news is emotion regulation can be learned at any age—through therapy, meditation, journaling, etc. We'll cover many such techniques in the next chapter.

It's also worth noting the role of resilience role models. Studies show that if you witness resilience in others (parents, mentors, even stories of famous survivors), it can bolster your own. It provides a blueprint in your mind that "if they could do it, maybe I can too." That's one reason we are drawn to stories of triumph (and why Chapter 9 highlights many)—they literally plant seeds of resilience in our psyche.

Introduction to Post-Traumatic Growth

A particularly hopeful area of research in resilience science is the study of post-traumatic growth (PTG). While we touched on this concept earlier, the scientific evidence deserves deeper exploration. Researchers Richard Tedeschi and Lawrence Calhoun have documented that between 50 and 80 percent of people who experience trauma report some form of positive change or growth as a result. These aren't just subjective feelings—the changes are often observable by friends and family members as well.

Their research has identified five key domains where this growth typically occurs:

1. **Greater appreciation for life and changed priorities**: People often report a heightened awareness of life's preciousness and a shift toward valuing relationships and meaningful experiences over material success or status.

2. **Improved relationships**: Many survivors develop deeper connections with others, increased compassion, and greater ease with vulnerability and intimacy.

3. **Recognition of new possibilities**: Trauma can lead to exploration of new paths, interests, or careers that might never have been considered otherwise.

4. **Enhanced personal strength**: The experience of surviving something difficult often leads to a greater sense of capability and self-reliance.

5. **Spiritual and existential growth**: Many people report deeper spiritual connections or more developed philosophical frameworks for understanding life.

Important to note is that post-traumatic growth doesn't occur instead of suffering—it happens alongside it. People who experience growth still feel pain, grief, and struggle. The growth emerges through the process of making meaning of the experience and integrating it into one's life narrative.

The science of PTG offers a powerful counter-narrative to the idea that trauma inevitably leads to permanent damage. While we should never minimize the very real suffering that trauma causes, research on PTG reminds us that human beings have remarkable capacity for transformation through even the most difficult experiences.

We'll explore the scientific evidence for this phenomenon in greater detail later in this chapter, examining both the conditions that foster such growth and its measurable effects on individuals' lives.

Social and Environmental Factors

Human beings are social creatures. Our resilience is deeply tied to our relationships. An oft-cited study of Harvard graduates (the Grant Study) found that the strongest predictor of well-being in later life was the quality of relationships. Connection fortifies us. In terms of pain and suffering, having people to turn to—friends, family, support groups—greatly reduces the mental toll. Loneliness and isolation, on the other hand, are like kryptonite to resilience. That's why one of the first things often recommended to someone in crisis is: don't isolate. Talk to someone. Accept help. Even talking to a professional counselor provides a human connection that can lighten the emotional load.

Communities can also be resilient or not. After natural disasters, some communities come together and rebuild effectively (think of how neighbors come together during a flood to help each other), while others might descend into chaos or conflict. Psychologists look at "community resilience"—factors like trust, leadership, and communication in a group that affect how well the whole community bounces back. We as individuals can seek out or foster resilient communities in our lives: supportive friend circles, workplaces with healthy culture, peer groups who share and listen.

I witnessed this community resilience firsthand during Venezuela's frequent power outages, which sometimes lasted for days. In my neighborhood, people who had rarely spoken before suddenly formed informal networks to share resources. One family with a gas stove would cook for several households. Another with a generator would offer phone charging. People who had stockpiled water shared with those who hadn't. What could have been a time of desperate competition became instead a demonstration of collective adaptation and mutual support. The experience taught me that resilience isn't just an individual quality—it can emerge at the level of entire communities when people connect and collaborate.

Another external factor: basic needs and safety. It's hard to be psychologically resilient if you're exhausted, starving, or in a physically unsafe situation. That's why part of building personal resilience can be very practical: improving sleep, nutrition, exercise, and secure housing if possible. These give your body-brain the resources to cope better. Think of a soldier: they go through physical training, not just mental, to handle stress. Similarly, exercise has been shown to improve mood and stress tolerance (it literally releases neurochemicals that make the brain more adaptive). Good sleep dramatically improves emotional regulation. So never underestimate the biology: sometimes the difference between despair and hope is a good meal and a good nap, as simple as that sounds.

Research at the University of California has shown that exercise increases the production of brain-derived neurotrophic factor (BDNF), a protein that promotes neural growth and protection. Higher BDNF levels are associated with improved mood, better learning, and protection against stress-related disorders. Even a single thirty-minute session of moderate exercise can elevate BDNF levels and improve cognitive function. This biological mechanism helps explain why so many resilient individuals instinctively turn to physical activity during times of stress—they're literally rebuilding their brain's capacity to adapt and thrive.

Cultural background can influence resilience too. Cultures that normalize talking about feelings might encourage seeking help, whereas more stoic cultures might encourage silent strength. There are strengths in each approach: silence can build inner fortitude, but reaching out can provide resources. The key is balance. If your culture values "never let them see you sweat," you might benefit from a trusted private outlet to express yourself. If your culture is very collective, you may have lots of support but maybe less practice standing on your own; you can work on personal coping skills. All humans have the capacity for resilience, but how we express and bolster it may vary.

Stress: Too Little, Too Much, Just Right

Earlier we mentioned stress inoculation and the idea of an optimal level of stress. Psychologists recognize that not all stress is bad. Some stress is called eustress (good stress)—like the butterflies before a big performance or the challenge that pushes you to grow. Too little stress (sustress) can actually weaken resilience because you never get to practice coping. Too much stress (distress) can overwhelm and damage. The goal is a balanced challenge. Think of it like weightlifting: lift too light and you gain no strength; lift way too heavy and you injure yourself; lift a challenging but doable weight and you grow stronger. Life works similarly.

Stanford psychologist Kelly McGonigal's research on the "upside of stress" demonstrates that how we think about stress matters tremendously. In one study, participants who were taught to view their stress response (racing heart, faster breathing) as their body preparing them to meet a challenge showed different physiological responses than those who viewed the same symptoms as harmful. The first group's blood vessels remained relaxed while their hearts worked harder—similar to what happens during moments of joy or courage. The second group showed the typical stress response of constricted blood vessels associated with chronic health problems. Simply changing the narrative around stress altered its physical impact.

The science of hormesis in biology echoes this: small doses of a toxin or stressor can be beneficial (like how vaccines work, or how intermittent fasting may improve cellular resistance, or how plants produce more antioxidants when slightly stressed by drought). With psychological stress, facing manageable challenges builds confidence and problem-solving skills for bigger ones.

That's why parents are advised not to overprotect children from every bump or failure—kids need to experience manageable setbacks to develop coping strategies. Likewise, as adults, we shouldn't overprotect ourselves from any discomfort. Taking on challenges like learning a new skill, engaging in sports, or traveling alone can build resilience "muscle" for when life throws more serious problems our way. It's a kind of self-training.

However, the science also shows the importance of recovery. Elite athletes have intense training but also strict rest days. Similarly, if you've gone through an especially traumatic period, you need a period of rest and recovery. You can't just push-push-push through life's hardships without burnout. Resilience involves knowing when to press forward and when to give yourself compassion and rest. Burnout and PTSD can result from chronic unrelenting stress. So building resilience is also about pacing—taking breaks, engaging in soothing activities (like hobbies, time in nature, and spiritual practices) to let your system recover. This is not a sign of weakness; it's strategic strength.

The Science of Post-Traumatic Growth

One of the most hopeful developments in resilience research is the growing body of evidence around post-traumatic growth (PTG). This term, coined by psychologists Richard Tedeschi and Lawrence Calhoun, describes the positive

THE POWER OF PAIN

psychological changes that can emerge from the struggle with highly challenging life circumstances. Their research has found that between 50-80% of people who experience trauma report some form of positive transformation as a result.

These aren't just subjective feelings—studies have documented measurable changes in values, behaviors, and life trajectories. For example, cancer survivors often report greater appreciation for life, closer relationships, and new priorities that outside observers can confirm. Research with military veterans has found that those who experience PTG show improved relationships and greater engagement in meaningful activities compared to pre-deployment.

The most compelling aspect of PTG research is that it doesn't deny suffering. People who experience growth still feel pain, grief, and struggle. The growth emerges through the process of trying to make sense of what happened and rebuilding one's life and identity afterward. This aligns perfectly with Viktor Frankl's insights about finding meaning in suffering, but now with substantial scientific validation.

Five domains where this growth typically occurs have been identified:

1. **Greater appreciation for life:** People often report a heightened awareness of life's preciousness and changed priorities.
2. **Improved relationships:** Many survivors develop deeper connections with others and greater compassion.
3. **New possibilities:** Trauma can lead to the exploration of new paths or interests.
4. **Enhanced personal strength:** The experience of surviving something difficult leads to greater confidence.
5. **Spiritual development:** Many people report deeper spiritual connections or more developed philosophical frameworks.

PTG research offers an evidence-based counter-narrative to the idea that trauma inevitably leads to permanent damage. While we should never minimize the very real suffering that trauma causes, the science of PTG reminds us that human beings have a remarkable capacity for transformation through even the most difficult experiences.

Putting Science into Practice

Understanding these scientific insights, we can be more deliberate in cultivating resilience:

- **Train your mindset:** Practice optimistic and growth-oriented thinking. This can literally rewire your brain's response to stress over time.

- **Build connections:** Nurture relationships and don't be afraid to lean on them during tough times. Social support is a huge resilience factor, proven over and over in studies.

- **Take care of your body:** Exercise, nutrition, and sleep fortify your brain's ability to handle stress. You produce more resilience neurotransmitters (like serotonin and endorphins) when you maintain physical health.

- **Face manageable challenges:** Step out of your comfort zone regularly in small ways. Learn something new or do something hard. It might stress you a bit, but in a good way that expands your capacity.

- **Practice stress-reduction techniques:** Techniques like deep breathing, meditation, or prayer can lower the physiological stress response. This can prevent acute stress from spiraling into trauma. It's like giving your body a reset signal.

- **Learn from resilient role models:** Read biographies or watch documentaries of individuals or communities that overcame the odds. This can inspire neurons in your brain to mirror that strength.

- **Have faith or belief:** Studies show that whether it's religious faith or a strong personal philosophy, believing in something greater than yourself or a larger meaning can buffer stress. It provides context and comfort when things go wrong.

Resilience is sometimes described as ordinary magic—because it's not about rare superhuman qualities, but rather ordinary things (like support, hope, and problem-solving) that any person can use. It can seem magical how people rebound, but it's usually thanks to these accessible factors. And remember, resilience doesn't mean you don't cry or break down; it means you eventually pick yourself up.

The science assures us that we are built to adapt. More than we often realize, our default as a species is to overcome. After all, humanity has survived floods, famines, wars, and migrations—and here we are. Each of us carries the genes of survivors. Our brains have systems to learn from pain and not only heal but improve (like immune systems that remember pathogens and guard better next time).

As we move into the next chapter on practical strategies, keep in mind that those techniques are effective in part because of the principles we've just discussed. When you practice reframing your thoughts, you are harnessing neuroplasticity and optimism. When you meditate, you are training your stress response. When you connect with a friend in hardship, you are leveraging social biology to regulate emotions. The why behind each strategy often lies in this science of resilience.

Pain-to-Power Exercises — Chapter 5

1. Resilience Timeline: Draw a horizontal line on a page representing your life. Mark several tough times you've been through. For each, jot down what factors helped you through it. Did you have supportive friends? Did you change how you thought about it? Did you engage in any activity that helped (like running, journaling, or prayer)? This will reveal what has worked for you in the past—your personal resilience factors. Recognizing these can remind you to use them for current or future challenges. You might discover, for example, that every time you faced loss, talking to your sister was key, or whenever you had work stress, your morning runs kept you sane. Those are your resilience habits; keep them close.

2. Build a Resilience Routine: Choose one scientifically backed resilience booster to incorporate into your routine for the next two weeks. Options include the following:

- Physical exercise: If you're not doing any, start with twenty minutes of walking or any activity you enjoy, most days of the week.
- Mindfulness meditation: Start with at least ten minutes a day of sitting quietly, focusing on your breath, or using a guided meditation app.
- Social connection: Schedule at least one meet-up or deep phone chat with a friend or relative per week.
- Skill challenge: Practice something slightly difficult daily, like a brain game, learning a language, or a hobby that challenges you.

Track your consistency. After two weeks, reflect on whether you feel any difference in your mood or stress levels. Most likely, you'll notice a positive change, which can motivate you to continue.

3. Resilient Role Model Research: Identify a person (famous or someone you know) whom you consider very resilient. Spend a little time researching or reflecting on what they went through and how they coped. If it's someone you know, perhaps even have a conversation with them about it. Write down two to three strategies or attitudes they used that you find inspiring. Next time you're in a tough situation, deliberately recall this role model and those strategies. For example, "My grandmother survived so much with grace; she always said her faith got her through. Maybe I can lean into my own form of faith or values now," or, "That marathon runner I read about used mantras when hitting the wall; I'll use a mantra to get through this challenge." Learning from others condenses hard-won wisdom into tools you can apply in your life.

Armed with both timeless wisdom and cutting-edge science, we're now ready to explore practical techniques that transform theory into action. The following chapter provides a toolkit of evidence-based strategies you can practically apply to your own challenges.

CHAPTER 6

Practical Strategies for Turning Pain into Power

From Theory to Practice – Building Your Resilience Toolkit

Having explored the theories and principles behind transforming suffering into strength, we now turn to practical application. This chapter offers concrete tools and techniques drawn from psychology, ancient wisdom traditions, and lived experience—a toolkit for resilience that anyone can implement in daily life. You don't need to adopt every strategy at once; even one or two practices can significantly shift your relationship with pain. Each method works not by helping you avoid or bury suffering, but by teaching you to observe it, soothe it, challenge it, and ultimately transform it into growth.

Building on the science we explored in chapter 5, we will now translate research findings into daily practices. The neuroplasticity that allows our brains to form new pathways after trauma can be deliberately activated through specific techniques. The stress regulation systems that determine our emotional resilience can be strengthened through consistent practice. The narrative frameworks that give meaning to our suffering can be consciously shaped through reflective exercises. In essence, we can learn to work with our brain's natural healing mechanisms rather than against them.

During my own exile journey, discovering these practices was transformative. They became my daily companions—anchors in the storm of displacement and reinvention. When language barriers frustrated me to the point of tears, mindfulness helped me create space between the emotion and my response to it. When loneliness for my homeland grew overwhelming, meaningful connection with others offered healing. When purpose seemed lost, journaling helped me rediscover it. These weren't just coping tricks; they were bridges from despair to possibility.

Let's explore these evidence-based approaches for transmuting pain into power, from mindfulness practices and cognitive reframing to self-compassion and meaningful action. By the end of this chapter, you'll have a menu of techniques you can incorporate into your life's routine. Over time, these practices will build your resilience, giving you the tools to cope with whatever life brings.

Mindfulness: Creating Space Between Pain and Response

When pain strikes—whether physical or emotional—our instinct is often to either fight against it or become completely identified with it. Both reactions typically intensify our suffering. Mindfulness offers a third path: we can observe our pain with compassionate awareness, creating crucial space between the sensation and our response to it.

During my second year in America, I experienced crippling anxiety as I struggled to build a new life. My mind raced constantly with worst-case scenarios—deportation, family members back home being harmed, complete financial collapse. One particularly difficult night, when sleep eluded me for the third night in a row, a friend from my homeland suggested a simple mindfulness practice she had learned. "Just focus on your breath," she said, "and when thoughts come, notice them without judgment and return to your breath." It sounded too simple to work, but desperation made me willing to try anything.

Sitting on the edge of my bed that night, I followed her instructions, focusing on the sensation of breathing while gently acknowledging the anxious thoughts that arose. "I notice I'm worrying about tomorrow's job interview . . . back to my breath." After about ten minutes, something shifted. The anxiety didn't disappear, but I created a small space between myself and the overwhelming feelings. I slept that night, and while it wasn't a miracle cure, it was my first experience of how mindfulness could change my relationship with pain.

Key Mindfulness Practices

Body Scan Meditation: Find a quiet place to sit or lie down. Starting from your toes and moving upward, bring attention to each part of your body. Notice any sensations—tension, warmth, tingling—without trying to change them. When you encounter areas of pain or discomfort, breathe into them with gentle awareness rather than resistance. This practice helps you develop the capacity to be present with discomfort without being overwhelmed by it.

RAIN Practice: When facing emotional pain, try this four-step process developed by meditation teacher Tara Brach:

- **R**ecognize what's happening. ("I'm feeling grief")
- **A**llow the experience to be there without fixing it.
- **I**nvestigate with kindness. (How does this feel in my body? What thoughts arise?)
- **N**urture yourself with self-compassion. (Place a hand on your heart and offer yourself words of comfort.)

Mindful Breathing: When stress or pain arises, pause and take five conscious breaths. Feel the sensation of air entering and leaving your body. Notice how your chest and abdomen move. This simple practice activates your parasympathetic nervous system, counteracting the stress response and creating momentary calm from which clearer thinking can emerge.

Thought Labeling: When painful thoughts dominate your mind, practice noticing and naming them: "Planning thought," "Worry thought," "Memory," "Judgment." This creates slight detachment from the thought content, helping you recognize that you are not your thoughts but the awareness observing them.

I practice mindful breathing before difficult phone calls with family in Venezuela, when news from home is particularly disturbing or when facing professional challenges in my new country. The practice doesn't eliminate problems but helps me approach them from a centered place rather than from panic or reactivity.

Cognitive Reframing: Changing the Story

Recall in earlier chapters we discussed the importance of mindset and the stories we tell ourselves. Cognitive reframing is a technique in cognitive-behavioral therapy (CBT) that you can practice to change your thoughts. The idea is to catch your automatic thoughts about a painful situation and then challenge and change them to be more constructive.

I vividly remember the day I received my first rejection letter from an American university where I had applied to continue my education. My immediate thought was, "I'll never succeed here. My English isn't good enough, and I don't belong in this country." This catastrophic interpretation sent me into a spiral of despair that lasted several days.

Eventually, a mentor suggested I try writing down my thoughts and examining them objectively. When I saw, "I'll never succeed here," on paper, I recognized how irrational it was. Had I really gathered enough evidence for "never"? Was one rejection letter proof of my entire future? Through this process, I gradually reframed my thought to, "This particular university didn't accept me, but that doesn't mean I won't find the right opportunity. My English is improving every day, and many immigrants before me have succeeded despite initial setbacks."

This reframed perspective didn't eliminate my disappointment, but it transformed it from debilitating to manageable. It gave me a path forward instead of a wall to crash against.

Practical Cognitive Reframing Techniques

Catch It, Check It, Change It: This three-step process helps you transform unhelpful thinking patterns:

1. **Catch** the negative thought in the act. Notice when you feel a wave of distress—what thought just went through your mind?
2. **Check** the thought: Is it an extreme? Is it catastrophizing? Is it personal? Would you say this to a good friend in your situation?
3. **Change** the thought to something more balanced or positive. If you identified distortions, correct them. You're not lying to yourself; you're telling the whole truth, which usually includes possibility and partial success.

Evidence Examination: When a painful thought arises ("I'm a failure," "No one cares about me," "This will never get better"), challenge it with evidence:

*   What facts contradict this thought?
*   What successes or positive experiences have you had, even small ones?
*   What might a neutral observer say about this situation?

Alternative Narrative Writing: When you're stuck in a negative story about a situation, deliberately write out three alternative interpretations. For example, if someone doesn't return your call and you think, "They're avoiding me because they don't like me," you might consider: "They're busy and haven't had time," "They might be dealing with their own challenges," "They might not have received my message."

Gratitude Reframing: Even amid difficulty, identify three things you're grateful for each day. This doesn't deny your pain but places it within a larger context that includes positive elements. Research shows this practice can shift your brain's default negativity bias over time.

I still use these techniques regularly. When news from Venezuela is troubling, when I face discrimination as an immigrant, or when professional challenges arise, I catch myself falling into catastrophic thinking and deliberately reframe my thoughts toward perspective and possibility.

Meaningful Connection: The Healing Power of Relationship

Humans are social creatures at our core. Neurologically, our brains and nervous systems regulate better in connection with others than in isolation. During times of suffering, reaching out rather than withdrawing can dramatically affect how we experience and process pain.

When I first arrived in America, pride and shame kept me isolated. I didn't want others to see me struggling with basic language or cultural norms. I pretended to understand conversations when I was lost, declined invitations rather than risk embarrassment, and projected false confidence while feeling deeply insecure. This isolation only intensified my suffering.

The turning point came when I reluctantly attended a community gathering for immigrants from various countries. There, I met María Elena from Colombia, who immediately recognized my Venezuelan accent and switched to Spanish. "It's hard at first, isn't it?" she said simply. Those words—acknowledging the difficulty without either minimizing or catastrophizing it—opened something in me. That evening I found myself sharing struggles I had kept hidden for months. The relief was palpable—not because my problems were solved, but because they were witnessed by someone who understood.

Connection Practices for Resilience

Vulnerability Courage: Choose one trusted person with whom you can be authentically honest about your struggles. Practice saying, "I'm having a hard time with . . ." without minimizing or exaggerating. Start small if this feels threatening, gradually building your capacity for vulnerable sharing.

Support Group Participation: Many communities have groups specifically for people facing similar challenges—grief, illness, addiction, immigration, parenting difficulties, etc. These groups provide both understanding and practical wisdom from others who have walked similar paths.

Helping Others: Paradoxically, supporting others facing similar challenges can strengthen your own resilience. When we offer compassion outward, we often internalize that same compassion for ourselves. Look for opportunities to volunteer, mentor, or simply listen to someone earlier in their journey than you.

Therapeutic Relationship: Professional mental health support can be invaluable during particularly difficult transitions. A skilled therapist provides both witness to your struggle and guidance for navigating it. I finally sought therapy three years into my American journey, and my only regret was not doing so sooner.

Digital Connection with Boundaries: When in-person connection isn't possible, digital communication can bridge gaps. Video calls have helped me maintain relationships with family and friends in Venezuela. However, be intentional about how you engage online, seeking meaningful exchange rather than passive scrolling that can increase isolation feelings.

I maintain connection through regular video calls with family in Venezuela, monthly dinners with fellow immigrants in my city, and participation in a writing group where we share stories of cultural transition. These communities don't eliminate my pain, but they make it more bearable by making it shared.

Emotional Expression: Giving Voice to Pain

Unexpressed emotions don't simply disappear; they go underground, often emerging later as physical symptoms, emotional numbness, or explosive reactions. Finding healthy channels for emotional expression helps process pain rather than being consumed by it.

For years after leaving Venezuela, I maintained a stoic facade, rarely allowing myself to express the grief and anger I felt. This suppression manifested as tension headaches, disrupted sleep, and occasional outbursts of irritability that confused those around me. I didn't want to burden others with my feelings, and part of me feared that if I started expressing grief, I might never stop.

A breakthrough came during a thunderstorm that reminded me powerfully of Caracas. Standing on my small apartment balcony, the tropical scent of rain-soaked earth triggered an overwhelming wave of homesickness. Instead of suppressing it as usual, I allowed myself to weep openly. The release was profound—not because it solved anything, but because it acknowledged the reality of my loss. I felt lighter afterward, more present, as if I had finally honored what was true instead of hiding from it.

Healthy Expression Practices

Journaling: Writing about painful experiences for fifteen to twenty minutes several times a week has been shown by research to improve both physical and mental health. Don't worry about grammar or structure; simply pour your thoughts and feelings onto the page without censorship. This practice externalizes internal suffering, helping you process and integrate difficult experiences.

Physical Release: Emotions live in our bodies, not just our minds. Physical activity can help release emotional energy—try running while visualizing leaving stress behind, punching a pillow to release anger safely, or dancing to express joy or grief. Notice where you hold tension (perhaps clenched jaw, tight shoulders, or constricted breathing) and deliberately release those areas.

Expressive Arts: Drawing, painting, music, dance, poetry—any creative outlet can provide a channel for emotions that might be difficult to articulate directly. You don't need artistic skill; the process itself is what matters. I began writing poetry about my immigration experience, finding that metaphor and imagery could capture nuances that direct description couldn't.

Verbal Expression: Sometimes we simply need to speak our truth aloud, whether to another person or even to an empty chair in a private moment. Naming our pain—"I feel abandoned," "I'm grieving what I lost," "I'm scared about the future"—helps us become more conscious of what we're experiencing and externalizes what may have been trapped inside.

Emotional Time Boundaries: Set aside specific times for focused emotional expression rather than trying to suppress feelings all day or letting them take over completely. I might designate Sunday evenings for looking at photos from home and allowing myself to feel the associated grief, knowing it has its place without dominating my entire week.

I now maintain a bilingual journal, writing in Spanish when processing deeper emotions about my homeland and in English when reflecting on my new life. This practice honors both worlds I inhabit and gives specific language to different aspects of my experience.

Meaning-Making: Finding Purpose in Pain

As we explored with Viktor Frankl's work, finding meaning in suffering can transform how we experience it. This doesn't mean pretending pain is good or that everything happens for a reason, but rather actively creating purpose from our difficult experiences.

One of my most challenging periods came about two years after arriving in America. I had achieved basic stability—a modest apartment, a steady job, improving English—yet I felt empty. The immediate survival concerns had receded, revealing a deeper question: What was it all for? Why continue this difficult journey of adaptation and constant effort? Without my homeland, my previous professional identity, and many of my relationships, what purpose remained?

This existential pain drove me to reflection. I began asking not just, "Why did this happen to me?" but, "What might I do with this experience?" Gradually, I recognized that my unique position as a Venezuelan in exile gave me perspective and voice that could serve others. What began as personal documentation about Venezuela's economic reality eventually evolved into DolarToday, providing crucial information to compatriots facing censorship. My suffering became meaningful not because it was inherently good, but because I found a way to use it in service of something larger than myself.

Meaning-Making Practices

Purpose Reflection: Ask yourself questions that connect your suffering to a larger meaning:

- What have I learned through this experience that I wouldn't have learned otherwise?
- How might my struggle help others facing similar challenges?
- What values or principles has this difficulty clarified for me?
- What might I be uniquely positioned to do or understand because of this experience?

Legacy Work: Consider how you want your response to suffering to affect others after you're gone. What example do you want to set? What lessons do you hope others will take from your journey? This perspective can elevate daily coping from mere survival to meaningful legacy building.

Values Clarification: Identify the core values that matter most to you (perhaps freedom, creativity, connection, integrity, etc.). Then explore how your response to current challenges might express and strengthen these values rather than contradicting them.

Helping Others: One of the most reliable paths to meaning is using your own experience to ease others' suffering. This might involve formal volunteering, informal mentoring, creating resources, or simply being present with compassion for someone facing what you've faced.

Ritual and Commemoration: Create meaningful rituals to honor difficult experiences. This might include lighting a candle on significant anniversaries, creating art that transforms pain into beauty, or establishing a tradition that commemorates loss while celebrating continuing life.

I practice meaning making by mentoring newer immigrants, documenting Venezuela's ongoing crisis from abroad, and using my bilingual voice to bridge cultural understanding. These pursuits don't erase my pain but give it purpose beyond mere personal suffering.

Self-Compassion: Being Your Own Best Friend

It's common in pain to beat ourselves up. We think, "I should be over this by now," or, "Why am I so weak?" But imagine a friend telling you they are hurting deeply. Would you scold them or call them weak? Probably not. You'd likely comfort them, assure them it's okay to feel that way, and maybe give a hug or words of support. Self-compassion is applying that same kindness to yourself.

When I first arrived in the United States, I was incredibly harsh with myself about my language limitations. I would internally berate myself for every grammatical mistake, every misunderstood conversation, and every awkward interaction. This self-criticism only increased my anxiety and slowed my learning. A turning point came when an ESL teacher suggested I speak to myself as I would to a friend learning a new language. "Would you mock a friend for mixing up verb tenses?" she asked. "Would you call them stupid for not knowing an idiom?" Of course not. When I began treating myself with this same compassion, not only did my mental health improve, but ironically, my English did too—fear and self-judgment had been blocking my learning.

Self-Compassion Practices

Mindful Self-Compassion Pause: When you notice self-criticism or overwhelming pain, try this brief practice developed by Kristin Neff:

1. Notice the suffering ("This is a moment of pain.")
2. Recognize our common humanity. ("Suffering is part of life; many others feel this way too.")
3. Offer yourself kindness. (Place a hand on your heart and speak to yourself gently.)

Compassionate Letter Writing: Write a letter to yourself from the perspective of an ideally compassionate friend who knows you completely, understands your situation, and feels unconditional love for you. What would this friend say about your struggles? How would they encourage you?

Self-Care Commitment: Identify concrete ways to care for yourself during difficult times, treating these commitments as seriously as you would promises to someone you love. This might include giving yourself adequate rest, nourishing food, movement, time in nature, creative expression, or spiritual practice.

Inner Critic Dialogue: When you notice harsh self-talk, try having a conversation with this critical voice. What is it afraid might happen if it weren't so hard on you? How might you respond with understanding while setting boundaries against its harshness?

Compassion Meditation: Practice a loving-kindness meditation, offering wishes for well-being first to yourself, then to loved ones, neutral people, difficult people, and finally all beings. This trains the mind to include you in the circle of compassion.

I practice self-compassion by maintaining a "self-kindness" note on my phone that I read when I'm being particularly hard on myself. It reminds me that adapting to a new country is objectively difficult, that my worth isn't determined by perfect English or immediate success, and that being patient with myself actually accelerates my growth rather than hinders it.

Somatic Approaches: Healing Through the Body

Trauma and emotional pain aren't just mental experiences; they live in our bodies. The nervous system holds patterns of tension, alarm, and shutdown that can persist long after danger has passed. Somatic (body-centered) approaches help regulate these physical patterns, creating safety and presence from the bottom up.

During my first years in exile, I experienced frequent physiological panic responses—racing heart, shallow breathing, cold sweats—particularly in situations where I felt exposed or inadequate. These weren't merely psychological reactions but deeply embodied responses to perceived threats. My body was constantly scanning for danger, a pattern established during the actual threats I had faced in Venezuela.

Discovering somatic approaches was transformative. I learned that by directly addressing my dysregulated nervous system through breath, movement, and awareness, I could create safety from the inside out. The first time I successfully used deep breathing to interrupt a panic attack before a job interview, I felt a profound shift in my relationship with fear. I couldn't change my external circumstances, but I could change how my body responded to them.

Somatic Healing Practices

Diaphragmatic Breathing: When stress activates, consciously shift to slow, deep breathing from your diaphragm rather than shallow chest breathing. Place one hand on your belly and feel it expand with each inhalation. Extended exhalations (longer than inhalations) activate the parasympathetic "rest and digest" system.

Grounding Techniques: When overwhelmed, connect to your physical environment through your senses. Try the 5-4-3-2-1 exercise: Notice 5 things you can see, 4 things you can touch, 3 things you can hear, 2 things you can smell, and 1 thing you can taste. This brings you back to the present moment when anxiety pulls you into the past or future.

Progressive Muscle Relaxation: Systematically tense and then release each muscle group in your body, starting from your toes and moving upward. This releases the physical tension we often don't even realize we're carrying and signals safety to the nervous system.

Embodied Movement: Gentle yoga, tai chi, dance, or even simply walking can help process emotions stored in the body. Notice where you hold tension and move in ways that create release. I found that merengue dancing—something familiar from my culture—both connected me to my roots and helped me release stress through rhythmic movement.

Therapeutic Touch: Safe, appropriate physical touch releases oxytocin, which counteracts stress hormones. This might be professional massage, hugs from trusted friends, or even self-touch like placing a hand over your heart during difficult moments.

I practice somatic regulation through a brief morning routine of gentle stretching and breath work, regular walks in nature, and dance classes that connect me to both my body and my cultural heritage. When anxiety arises, I immediately shift to deep breathing and physical grounding before addressing the mental content of my worry.

Creating a Personalized Resilience Routine

After reviewing all these strategies, it might be helpful to create a resilience routine for yourself. This is a set of daily or weekly practices you commit to to maintain and build your mental and emotional strength. For example, your routine could look like this: morning meditation for ten minutes, journaling in the evening for ten minutes, exercising (jogging or yoga, for example) three times a week, and making a gratitude list each night. Create this routine around what works for you. The key is consistency—just like muscles need regular exercise, resilience skills do too.

My own resilience routine evolved through trial and error. I found that prayer in the morning centered me for the day, while journaling before bed helped me process the day's events. On Sundays, I made a point of calling family in Venezuela to maintain those crucial connections. I also discovered that even brief periods of exercise—just twenty minutes of running—dramatically improved my mood and thinking clarity when I felt overwhelmed. These weren't random activities but a deliberate pattern that supported my mental, emotional, and spiritual well-being through challenging times.

Building Your Personalized Routine

Start Small: Begin with just one or two practices that resonate most strongly with you. It's better to do one thing consistently than to attempt an elaborate routine you can't maintain. Perhaps begin with just five minutes of mindful breathing each morning or a brief gratitude practice before bed.

Stack Habits: Connect new resilience practices to existing habits. For example, practice mindful breathing while waiting for your morning coffee to brew, or do a brief body scan before your shower. This *habit stacking* makes integration into daily life more seamless.

Track Consistency: Use a simple tracking system (like marking a calendar or using a habit app) to record your practice consistency. This provides both accountability and the satisfaction of seeing your commitment visually represented.

Reassess Regularly: Every month, take a few minutes to reflect on your resilience practice. What's working well? What feels forced or ineffective? Be willing to adjust your routine as you learn more about what specifically supports your resilience.

Balance Structure and Flexibility: While consistency matters, avoid rigidity. Some days you might need more of one practice than another. Learn to listen to what your mind and body need in a given moment while maintaining the overall structure that supports you.

Include Connection: Ensure your routine includes regular connection with supportive others. Resilience isn't a solo project; it flourishes in community. Schedule regular check-ins with friends, family, or support groups who understand your journey.

It's understandable if at first you don't feel like doing these things. Pain can sap motivation. But start tiny—write one paragraph in your journal do two minutes of deep breathing, walk one lap around the block. The important thing is to start. Often, the motivation follows action, not the other way around.

When to Seek Help

While self-help strategies are incredibly valuable, seeking professional help is a powerful strategy too. If your pain—be it depression, trauma, chronic pain syndrome, etc.—is overwhelming despite your best efforts, reaching out to a therapist, counselor, or support group is a sign of strength, not weakness. These professionals can offer tools that complement what you're doing on your own.

When I finally sought therapy three years after arriving in America, I was surprised to discover I had been experiencing PTSD symptoms without recognizing them. My therapist offered specialized techniques for trauma processing that I couldn't have learned from books or friends, however supportive they were.

Seeking professional help wasn't admitting defeat—it was adding another powerful tool to my resilience toolkit.

Signs That Professional Help Would Be Beneficial

- Your daily functioning is significantly impaired (sleep, appetite, work, relationships).
- You've tried self-help strategies consistently without improvement.
- You're using substances or other behaviors to numb your pain.
- You have thoughts of suicide or not wanting to live.
- The same painful patterns keep repeating despite your efforts to change them.
- Your support network is limited or unavailable.
- Your pain stems from complex trauma that requires specialized approaches.

The goal of all these strategies, whether self-administered or with help, is to empower you, to make you feel that you have tools in your toolbox when pain comes knocking. Instead of saying, "Oh no, I can't handle this," when challenges arise, you might find yourself saying, "This is hard, but I have ways to deal with it. I've done it before, and I can do it again."

As you continue to practice and refine these strategies, you will likely notice a shift: things that used to break you now only bend you; what once felt unbearable becomes, if not pleasant, at least something you can carry with confidence and grace. That is the essence of turning pain into power—you become stronger than your struggles.

Pain-to-Power Exercises – Chapter 6

1. Daily Mindfulness or Prayer Micro-Practice: Start a habit of doing one centering exercise per day. This could be doing a mindfulness practice like five minutes of focused breathing, praying one decade of the Rosary (about five minutes), or repeating the Jesus Prayer for several minutes. Track this practice with a habit tracker or a tick on your calendar each day you do it. After one week, reflect in your journal on the following: do you notice any difference in your overall stress or how you reacted to something upsetting? This micro-practice builds your ability to create space between stimulus and response—a fundamental skill for transforming pain. Even brief daily practice strengthens the mental muscle that allows you to respond to difficulty with presence rather than reactivity.

2. Thought Reframe Worksheet: Take a sheet of paper and draw two columns. Label one "Painful Thought" and the other "Reframe/Response." Over the next few days, whenever you catch a negative, painful thought, jot it down (e.g., "I'll never get better from this."). In the second column, actively write a kinder or more hopeful reframing (e.g., "Healing takes time. I have gotten through difficult things before, so there's reason to hope I will improve."). At the end of the week, read through the list of reframes. This cognitive exercise helps you develop the habit of challenging catastrophic thinking and replacing it with more balanced perspectives, reducing the emotional suffering that comes from distorted thoughts.

3. Self-Care Menu: Create a personal self-care menu to use when you're in pain. Divide a page into five sections and label them "Physical," "Emotional," "Mental," "Social," and "Spiritual." Under each, list a few go-to soothing or uplifting activities. For example: Physical (take a warm bath, do ten minutes of stretching), Emotional (listen to a favorite song, cry if I need to, cuddle a pet), Mental (read an inspiring article, do a puzzle), Social (call a friend, or post in my support group online), Spiritual (pray, meditate in nature). Next time you're overwhelmed by pain or stress, pull out this menu and choose one activity from any category to do. This proactive approach to self-care ensures you don't have to think of coping strategies when you're already overwhelmed—they're ready when you need them.

Having explored how adversity can strengthen us, let's shift our focus to athletics, where athletes deliberately expose themselves to mental, emotional, and physical challenges in pursuit of achievement. While previous chapters examined how we respond to unavoidable suffering, the world of athletes offers a unique model of voluntarily engaging with difficulty. Their journeys show how we can embrace discomfort by approaching it with purpose, to turn pain into strength and achievement.

CHAPTER 7

The Athlete's Crucible

Transforming Sweat Into Glory

The Sacrifice Behind Every Victory

In my first year in America, seeking release from the stress of exile, I found myself in a boxing gym. One evening, exhausted from language drills and low-wage work, I watched a young fighter training through obvious pain. "Pain forges strength from weakness!" his coach called out as the fighter pushed through his final repetitions, face contorted but determined. In that moment, I recognized something profound about athletic discipline that spoke directly to my own circumstances. The voluntary embrace of difficulty—the deliberate seeking of challenge and even pain—could forge a strength that might otherwise remain dormant. While my challenges weren't physical in the same way, the boxer's relationship with suffering revealed a universal truth: our capacity to grow is often directly proportional to our willingness to endure discomfort with purpose.

Athletic achievement offers perhaps our clearest model of how suffering, approached with intention, builds extraordinary capacity. From ancient Olympic competitors to modern-day elite athletes, those who excel in sport demonstrate the extraordinary capacity of human beings to convert physical pain, psychological pressure, and devastating setbacks into transcendent achievement. Their journeys offer powerful lessons for anyone seeking to transform any form of suffering into strength.

"No Pain, No Gain."

This simple phrase, plastered on gym walls worldwide, captures a fundamental truth about athletic achievement: significant advancement requires significant discomfort. What spectators witness—the glorious touchdown, the perfect dismount, the record-breaking sprint—represents just the visible peak of an immense iceberg of voluntary suffering that lies beneath.

Michael Jordan, widely considered basketball's greatest player, was once asked about his extraordinary success. He replied, "I've missed more than nine thousand shots in my career. I've lost almost three hundred games. Twenty-six times I've been trusted to take the game-winning shot and missed. I've failed over and over and over again in my life. And that is why I succeed." This revealing statement highlights the repeated disappointments, failures, and setbacks that precede athletic greatness—experiences that would be classified as suffering in any other context but in athletics become the necessary crucible for transformation.

What makes athletic pain transformative rather than merely destructive? Several distinctive elements emerge:

Voluntary Discomfort: Unlike many forms of suffering, athletic pain is largely chosen rather than merely endured. This element of choice transforms the relationship with discomfort. As ultramarathon champion David Goggins explains, "When you choose to suffer, you're in control of the pain." This sense of agency—deciding when, how, and why to subject oneself to difficulty—creates a fundamentally different psychological relationship with suffering than when pain is entirely unwanted or unexpected.

I experienced this distinction during my military training in Venezuela and later during my immigrant journey. In training, I chose difficulty, understanding its purpose. The suffering had meaning and boundaries. In exile, many hardships were thrust upon me without my consent. Learning to reclaim a sense of choice within forced circumstances—to voluntarily embrace challenges like language learning or cultural adaptation—helped transform my relationship with suffering from victim to agent.

Progressive Overload: Athletic training follows the principle that growth requires systematically increasing demands beyond current capacity. Muscles don't strengthen from comfortable exertion but from being pushed slightly beyond their current limits, creating microtears that heal stronger than before. This same principle applies to cardiovascular capacity, skill development, and mental toughness. Athletes and coaches carefully calibrate discomfort, seeking the optimal stress level that promotes maximal growth—challenging enough to stimulate adaptation but not so severe as to cause breakdown.

Directed Purpose: Athletic suffering isn't random or pointless; it's precisely targeted toward specific improvements. A gymnast endures the pain of thousands of repetitions to perfect a single movement. A hockey player embraces the discomfort of early morning practices to develop team coordination. This clear connection between present pain and future achievement creates meaning that transforms suffering from something to be survived into something purposefully embraced.

Trusted Guidance: Behind most athletic achievements is a coach, mentor, or training methodology that directs the suffering toward productive rather than destructive ends. This guidance ensures that pain serves development rather than causing damage. Coaches know when to push and when to permit recovery, when suffering builds character and when it merely breaks bodies.

These elements—choice, progression, purpose, and guidance—create the conditions for athletic suffering to become transformative rather than destructive. They don't eliminate pain but rather convert it from enemy to ally, from obstacle to opportunity.

Physical Pain as the Forge of Excellence

Physical discomfort in athletics takes many forms: the burning lungs of cardiovascular exertion, the trembling muscles of strength training, the blistered hands of gymnastic preparation, and the impact injuries of contact sports. These sensations, which in other contexts might signal danger, are feedback to the athlete that transformation is occurring.

What makes physical pain productive rather than merely harmful? Science reveals several key principles:

Supercompensation: Athletic development follows a cycle of stress, recovery, and adaptation. When muscles or cardiovascular systems experience appropriate stress, they initially weaken (breakdown phase). With adequate recovery time and nutrition, they rebuild to a capacity slightly beyond their original state (supercompensation). This biological principle—that systems return stronger after stress—forms the foundation of physical training.

Pain Differentiation: Athletes develop a sophisticated awareness of different pain types. The "good pain" of productive training (temporary, diminishing with rest, symmetrical) signals adaptation. The "bad pain" of potential injury (sharp, persistent, asymmetrical) signals danger. Knowing which pain to push through and which to respect prevents destructive suffering while embracing productive discomfort.

Elite athletes develop remarkable relationships with physical pain. Distance runner Emil Zátopek, known for his punishing training regimens, explained, "If you want to win something, run 100 meters. If you want to experience something, run a marathon." He understood that greater physical discomfort opened door to deeper experiences unavailable to those who prioritize comfort.

My own experience testing my physical limits began in Venezuelan military training, where I learned that my body could endure far more than my mind initially believed possible. These lessons proved valuable during my immigrant journey, when my new job required strenuous physical labor. The willingness to embrace physical discomfort—standing for long shifts at retail jobs, performing manual labor despite my education—sustained me while I rebuilt my professional life.

The Champion's Mindset: Mental Toughness Through Adversity

"The body achieves what the mind believes." This athletic wisdom acknowledges that physical performance is inseparable from mental frameworks. While physical pain represents one dimension of athletic suffering, the psychological challenges often prove even more demanding: performance anxiety, competitive pressure, fear of failure, motivational struggles, and the mental strain of pushing beyond perceived limitations.

Champions develop distinctive mental approaches that transform these psychological challenges into fuel for achievement. These approaches include the following:

Reframing Pain: Elite athletes learn to interpret pain signals not as warnings to stop but as indicators of productive effort. Marathon runners describe "embracing the hurt" rather than resisting it. Weight lifters welcome the burning sensation of muscle fatigue as evidence of growth stimulation. This cognitive reframing doesn't deny pain's existence but transforms its meaning from threat to progress marker.

During language acquisition, I learned to reframe the mental fatigue and social anxiety of speaking English. Instead of interpreting these uncomfortable feelings as signals to retreat to my native Spanish, I began seeing them as evidence that I was expanding my capabilities—the "burn" that preceded fluency. This athletic mindset helped me push through the temptation to avoid uncomfortable conversations.

Compartmentalization: Athletes develop the capacity to separate pain from performance, focusing attention on execution rather than discomfort. Tennis champion Novak Djokovic describes playing through injuries by "putting pain in a box" mentally—acknowledging its presence but refusing to allow it to dominate his awareness. This compartmentalization doesn't eliminate suffering but prevents it from consuming all attentional resources.

This mental skill proved invaluable to me when I was balancing multiple life challenges simultaneously during my adaptation to the United States. I had to compartmentalize homesickness to focus on work, set aside status anxiety to concentrate on education, and contain financial stress to maintain creative energy for writing and activism. Like an athlete playing through pain, I learned to acknowledge these difficulties without letting them hinder my performance.

Adversity as Advantage: Many champions deliberately recast obstacles as opportunities. Basketball legend Kobe Bryant, reflecting on his Achilles tendon rupture, noted, "The injury helped me discover new areas of my game." Rather than viewing setbacks merely as disadvantages, elite competitors actively seek the hidden advantages within limitations. This perspective shift transforms obstacles from purely negative experiences into potential pathways to innovation.

Process Orientation: While goal achievement motivates athletes, champions develop a profound focus on the process rather than outcomes. They concentrate on executing the next move perfectly rather than obsessing about the final results. This process orientation makes overwhelming challenges manageable by reducing them to discrete, controllable actions in the present moment.

NBA coach Phil Jackson, known for his psychological approach to developing champions, observed, "The most we can hope for is to create the best possible conditions for success, then let go of the outcome." This mindset of controlling what can be controlled, accepting what cannot, and continuing forward regardless represents the essence of athletic mental toughness.

These mental approaches aren't merely theoretical concepts but are vividly demonstrated in the remarkable comeback stories of athletes who have faced devastating setbacks yet found their way back to excellence. Their journeys illustrate how the champion's mindset translates into tangible resilience when confronted with career-threatening challenges.

Rising from Defeat: Remarkable Athletic Comebacks

Some of sport's most inspiring stories center on comebacks—times when athletes faced career-threatening defeats, devastating injuries, or public failures yet returned to achieve what seemed impossible. The following are some of these stories.

Monica Seles

Tennis champion Monica Seles was at the peak of her career in 1993 when a deranged fan stabbed her during a match. The physical wound healed relatively quickly, but the psychological trauma kept her from competition for over two years. Many experts believed her career was effectively over. Yet Seles ultimately returned to win another Grand Slam title, demonstrating extraordinary emotional and physical resilience.

Her comeback required physical rehabilitation as well as confronting her fear, shattered assumptions about safety, and having lost prime competitive years. Seles later reflected, "I had to accept that I would never be the same player or person again—but that didn't mean I couldn't be strong in new ways." This insight—that resilience isn't about returning to an unchanged previous state but about creating new strength—reflects a sophisticated understanding of how suffering transforms rather than merely interrupts.

Like Seles, I had to accept that exile meant I would never be exactly the same person I was in Venezuela. Rather than trying in vain to return to my previous identity, I needed to integrate my experiences into a new, more complex self. This perspective helped me focus on developing new strengths rather than merely mourning what was lost.

Tiger Woods

Tiger Woods's comeback journey offers another great example of transformation through multiple forms of suffering. After reaching unprecedented dominance in golf, Woods experienced a combination of physical injuries, personal scandals, and performance collapse that seemed to end his elite career. His world ranking plummeted from #1 to #1,199. Yet in 2019, after multiple back surgeries and years of struggle, Woods won the Masters tournament again—a victory *Sports Illustrated* called "the greatest comeback in sports history."

Woods's journey is relevant to many because he experienced multiple dimensions of suffering: physical pain (spinal fusion surgery), public humiliation (widely publicized personal failings), identity crisis (loss of dominance in the arena that defined him), and the psychological challenge of rebuilding confidence from scratch. His eventual triumph required not just physical rehabilitation but comprehensive transformation—a journey from rock bottom to newfound strength.

I personally found inspiration in athletic comebacks like these during particularly difficult periods of my adaptation to America. When language barriers seemed insurmountable, when professional rejection felt permanent, and when cultural disorientation threatened my sense of self, stories of athletes who had overcome more dramatic setbacks provided both perspective and practical models for persistence.

Team Resilience: Collective Strength after Failure

While individual athletic journeys demonstrate personal resilience, team sports reveal how shared suffering can forge collective strength. Teams that weather devastating losses, overcome internal conflict, or face external obstacles together often develop bonds and capabilities unavailable to those who haven't experienced collective hardship.

The 2016 Cleveland Cavaliers made NBA history as the first team ever to overcome a 3-1 deficit in the Finals, defeating the heavily favored Golden State Warriors. Their journey involved not just the immediate series deficit but also years of Cleveland's infamous sports disappointments and internal team chemistry challenges. Forward LeBron James reflected, "The hard road makes the end result that much sweeter. It builds something in you that cannot be developed through success alone."

This observation highlights a paradox of team development: while coaches and organizations naturally seek victory, teams often develop their most significant cohesion and character through collective struggle rather than uninterrupted success. The shared vulnerability of facing potential failure, the trust required to persevere together, and the mutual accountability developed through adversity create bonds that mere talent alignment cannot produce.

In building community among Venezuelan exiles in America, I witnessed similar dynamics. Our shared experience of displacement, loss, and adaptation created connections far deeper than casual association. The collective processing of national trauma and the mutual support through individual challenges forged a resilient community that would have been impossible without shared suffering. Like an athletic team that had weathered losses together, we developed special strength through collective hardship.

The key elements that transform collective suffering into team strength include the following:

- **Shared vulnerability:** When team members witness each other struggling—seeing both limitations and the commitment to push through them—deeper trust develops than when only strengths are visible.
- **Meaningful narrative:** Teams that develop compelling stories about their challenges, framing difficulties as part of a larger purpose, maintain motivation and cohesion through extended adversity.
- **Distributed resilience:** Strong teams develop complementary coping mechanisms, with different members providing strength during different phases of challenge—creating resilience greater than any individual could maintain.
- **Collective identity:** Navigating adversity together creates a distinct "us" separate from those who haven't shared the experience—a powerful bonding force that fuels future performance.

Beyond the Arena: Athletic Discipline in Everyday Challenges

The principles that transform athletic suffering into achievement apply far beyond sports contexts. Whether facing health challenges, career setbacks, relationship difficulties, or the specific pains of displacement and adaptation, the athlete's approach to adversity offers a template for productive engagement with suffering of all kinds.

Three-time cancer survivor and ultramarathon champion Don Wright embodies this extension of athletic principles beyond conventional competition. Diagnosed with multiple myeloma at age sixty-two and given just three to five years to live, Wright began running marathons during cancer treatment. Seventeen years later, having completed marathons in all fifty states while continually undergoing chemotherapy, Wright demonstrates how athletic engagement with suffering transcends sport itself.

"Running marathons and fighting cancer require the same mindset," Wright explains. "You break the overwhelming challenge into smaller segments, you focus on the present moment rather than the total distance, you expect pain but don't let it define your experience, and you maintain absolute belief in your ability to reach the finish line regardless of current difficulties."

His approach illustrates how athletic principles—breaking challenges into manageable segments, focusing on process rather than being overwhelmed by the total journey, expecting difficulty as part of achievement, and maintaining belief through temporary setbacks—apply directly to life's most serious challenges.

When I faced the overwhelming process of rebuilding my life in a new country, I instinctively applied these same athletic principles—breaking the massive challenge into smaller segments like language acquisition, education, professional development, and community building. Rather than being paralyzed by the total distance between my starting point and desired destination, I focused on the immediate "mile markers" along the journey.

Cancer survivor and Paralympic gold medalist Oksana Masters provides another powerful example of athletic principles applied to extreme life challenges. Born with radiation-induced birth defects in Ukraine following the Chernobyl disaster, Masters spent her early years in orphanages before being adopted by an American mother. She endured multiple surgeries, including double leg amputation.

Rather than being defined by these extraordinary difficulties, Masters applied athletic discipline to become a multi-sport Paralympic champion in rowing, cycling, biathlon, and cross-country skiing. She describes the transformation: "Being an athlete taught me that pain always has a purpose. In competition, pain means you're pushing limits. In recovery from surgery, pain means you're healing. Either way, pain isn't your enemy—it's information about a process that's happening."

This perspective—pain as information about a process rather than merely a negative experience to avoid—reflects the athlete's sophisticated relationship with discomfort. It applies equally to physical rehabilitation, emotional healing, professional challenges, or adaptation to radical life changes.

The athlete's approach to suffering offers particular value for several common life challenges:

- **Health crises:** Patients who apply athletic principles to medical challenges—viewing treatment as training, recovery as a competitive event with distinct phases, and setbacks as temporary rather than definitive—often demonstrate better psychological coping and sometimes even improved medical outcomes.

- **Career transitions:** Job loss, professional reinvention, or workplace challenges become more navigable when approached with the athlete's focus on preparation, process orientation, and growth through difficulty rather than mere avoidance of discomfort.

- **Relationship difficulties:** The athlete's understanding that growth requires stress applies to emotional challenges as well. Relationships that avoid all conflict ultimately lack resilience, while those that face difficulties head-on with purpose and appropriate boundaries often become deeper.

- **Educational challenges:** Students who approach learning difficulties with the athlete's expectation that mastery requires productive struggle rather than ease demonstrate greater academic resilience and ultimately deeper understanding than those who interpret struggle as evidence of inadequacy.

As someone who found himself in an entirely new country, culture, and career path, I've come to see my immigrant journey as an ultra-endurance event—one requiring pacing for the long term, an expectation of difficulty as part of the course, a celebration of small milestones along the way, and absolute commitment to reaching the finish line regardless of temporary setbacks. This athletic framing has transformed how I experience the suffering that comes with adaptation, seeing it as productive rather than merely painful.

Pain-to-Power Exercises – Chapter 7

1. Reframing Pain Journal: For one week, keep a daily log of uncomfortable experiences (physical discomfort, emotional stress, challenging situations). For each entry, practice the athlete's reframing by answering three questions:

- What specific discomfort am I experiencing? (Be precise about the sensation or feeling.)
- What might this discomfort be teaching or developing in me?
- How might I view this as productive rather than merely negative?

Review your entries at week's end to identify patterns in how you experience and interpret discomfort. Notice which reframes feel most authentic and helpful for your specific challenges. This exercise helps you develop the athlete's mindset that interprets pain as productive feedback rather than just something to avoid.

2. Progressive Challenge Design: Identify an area of your life where growth requires embracing rather than avoiding discomfort (perhaps public speaking, difficult conversations, physical fitness, or language learning). Design a six-week progressive challenge program that gradually increases difficulty at an optimal rate—challenging enough to stimulate growth but not so overwhelming that you won't continue it. Include specific benchmarks, recovery periods, and success metrics. This exercise applies the athletic principle of progressive overload to personal development, helping you systematically build capacity by deliberately engaging with increasing levels of challenge rather than simply trying to avoid discomfort.

3. Mental Performance Routine: Develop a pre-challenge routine for situations you find difficult (job interviews, medical procedures, interpersonal conflicts). Following the athlete's model, create a specific sequence of physical actions (controlled breathing, posture adjustment), mental focus (attention cues, visualization), and emotional centering (purpose reminder, confidence statement). Practice this routine daily for two weeks, then apply it before your next challenging situation. This exercise provides a psychological structure for transforming anxiety into focused performance, just as athletes use routines to center themselves before competition. By creating a consistent pre-challenge ritual, you develop a reliable method for accessing your best self precisely when challenges are most difficult.

Athletes show us how physical pain builds bodily strength, but suffering can also catalyze spiritual development. Let's now explore how various wisdom traditions understand pain as a potential doorway to expanded consciousness and deeper connection with life, examining practices that transform lead into gold within the human spirit.

CHAPTER 8

The Spiritual Alchemy
of Suffering

Transmuting Pain into Spiritual Gold

Sitting in silent meditation at a ten-day retreat, I faced a pain in my knee that seemed unbearable. Every fiber of my being wanted to move, to escape, to find relief. The teacher had instructed us to observe sensations without reacting— easy to say, nearly impossible to do. Yet as I continued to sit, something remarkable happened. As I stopped fighting the pain and simply witnessed it with detached calmness, the experience transformed. The pain remained, but my relationship to it shifted dramatically. What had been torture became teaching. In that moment, I glimpsed what mystics across traditions have discovered: pain can be a doorway to deeper consciousness, and suffering, while never sought, can be alchemized into spiritual growth.

Throughout human history, spiritual traditions have grappled with the meaning and purpose of suffering. While science explains how pain works and psychology examines our mental responses to it, spirituality asks deeper questions: What is the soul-level purpose of our pain? How might suffering be a catalyst for awakening? This chapter explores how various wisdom traditions understand the spiritual dimensions of pain and offers practices to alchemize suffering into expanded awareness and deeper connection with life.

The process is akin to alchemy—the ancient practice of turning base metals into gold. While physical alchemy may remain elusive, spiritual alchemy is very real. It is the inner work of transmuting the lead of our suffering into the gold of wisdom, compassion, and awakened presence.

The Dark Night of the Soul: Transformation Through Crisis

The phrase *dark night of the soul* comes from a poem by sixteenth-century mystical poet St. John of the Cross, describing a profound spiritual crisis where one feels utterly abandoned by God. Today, we use this term more broadly to describe periods of intense inner suffering, questioning, and disorientation that ultimately lead to spiritual awakening. These dark nights are not merely bad moods or temporary setbacks—they are profound existential crises that challenge our identity and understanding of life.

Thomas Moore, psychotherapist and author of "Dark Nights of the Soul," writes that these periods "are opportunities to grow and become more sensitive to life's mysteries." The dark night strips away our illusions, our attachments, and sometimes even our faith, leaving us raw and vulnerable. However, this vulnerability creates an opening for profound transformation. When everything we believed about life or ourselves comes undone, we enter a fertile void where new understanding can emerge.

This pattern of transformation through darkness appears across spiritual traditions. In Buddhism, the Buddha's journey through extreme asceticism before finding the Middle Way represents such a passage. In Islamic Sufism, the concept of *fana* (annihilation of the separate self) precedes *baqa* (subsistence in God). Indigenous traditions include vision quests where isolation and physical hardship precede spiritual revelation. While the specifics differ, the common thread is clear: periods of profound disorientation and suffering often precede spiritual awakening.

In my own experience, leaving my homeland, under threat, I entered a dark night. Everything familiar was stripped away—my home, profession, identity, language, and community. I felt profound loss and disorientation. Yet in that darkness, when all external supports fell away, I discovered inner resources I never knew existed. A resilience emerged from somewhere deeper than my personality. Many spiritual teachers suggest that's exactly the point of the dark night—to force us beyond our limited self-construct into a more authentic relationship with life.

How do we navigate these dark passages? First, we must recognize them for what they are. Rather than merely personal failure or bad luck, these periods can be understood as sacred initiations. Second, we must surrender to the process, not fight it. Resistance only prolongs the night. Third, we must find appropriate support—whether spiritual directors, therapists who understand spiritual dimensions, or communities that honor these transitions. Finally, we must trust the darkness itself—knowing that throughout human history, the dark night has been recognized as the prelude to greater light.

As Leonard Cohen sang, "There is a crack in everything—that's how the light gets in." Our brokenness becomes the very opening through which transformation enters.

Ancient Wisdom for Modern Wounds: Meditative Approaches to Pain

Throughout history, contemplative traditions have developed sophisticated methods for working with pain—not only to reduce suffering but to transform it into a path of awakening. These approaches remain remarkably relevant for our modern challenges, offering time-tested wisdom for physical, emotional, and existential pain.

The Rosary: Rhythmic Prayer and Meditation

During the darkest days of my exile from Venezuela, when I felt utterly alone despite being surrounded by people, I rediscovered a practice from my childhood:

praying the Rosary. My grandmother had taught me this sequence of prayers when I was young, but I had drifted away from it in adulthood. On those difficult nights in a strange country, the familiar rhythm of the Hail Marys and Our Fathers became a lifeline. The repetitive nature of the prayers quieted my racing mind while I meditated on the Sorrowful Mysteries—Christ's suffering before crucifixion—and gave my pain context and meaning. I wasn't praying to escape my suffering but to find strength within it, just as Jesus had done.

The Rosary is an ancient Christian devotional practice dating back at least to the Middle Ages. It consists of a series of prayers recited in sequence, typically using beads to track progress. The physical beads provide a tactile focus, while the repetitive prayers create a meditative rhythm that calms the mind and opens the heart.

What makes the Rosary particularly relevant to transforming pain is its incorporation of the "mysteries"—key events in the lives of Jesus and Mary that practitioners contemplate while praying. The Sorrowful Mysteries focus on Christ's suffering—his agony in the garden, scourging, crowning with thorns, carrying of the cross, and crucifixion. By meditating on these events while praying, one places personal suffering in conversation with sacred suffering, finding meaning and companionship in pain rather than isolation.

The neurological benefits of praying the Rosary have been documented in scientific research. Studies show that the rhythmic breathing and repetitive prayers create a coherent heart rate pattern similar to that found in meditation, reducing stress hormones and enhancing immune function. The practice also activates the parasympathetic nervous system—our *rest-and-digest* response—countering the sympathetic *fight-or-flight* activation that chronic pain and suffering often trigger.

The Jesus Prayer: Centering the Heart

Another profound prayer practice comes from the Eastern Orthodox tradition: the Jesus Prayer. This simple prayer—"Lord Jesus Christ, Son of God, have mercy on me, a sinner"—has been practiced continuously since at least the fifth century, particularly by monks and mystics in the Christian East. Also known as the Prayer of the Heart, it forms the core of *hesychasm*, an ancient approach to contemplative prayer.

What makes the Jesus Prayer so powerful for transforming pain is its ultimate goal: to move from being a prayer one says to a prayer that says itself continuously in the heart, becoming as natural as breathing. Orthodox practitioners traditionally repeat the prayer thousands of times daily, often coordinated with the breath (inhaling with, "Lord Jesus Christ, Son of God," and exhaling with, "have mercy on me, a sinner") until it becomes internalized in what they call "the prayer of the heart."

During a particularly difficult period when I was battling deep uncertainty about my future in America, a Russian Orthodox friend taught me this practice. What struck me was how the prayer's emphasis on mercy created a profound shift in my relationship with suffering. Instead of fighting against pain or begging for its removal, the prayer fostered an attitude of receptivity to divine mercy within the present moment, however difficult that moment might be.

Both the Rosary and the Jesus Prayer share important elements with mindfulness meditation while adding the dimension of divine relationship. Both practices focus attention rather than allowing the mind to ruminate on pain, create rhythm through repetition that calms the nervous system, connect individual suffering to a larger context of meaning, and activate embodied awareness through breath and physical elements.

Mindfulness Meditation: Befriending Pain

Mindfulness meditation, with roots in Buddhist practice, teaches us to observe pain directly without the additional suffering of resistance, fear, or storylines. When we experience pain (physical or emotional), we typically react in one of two ways: we either try to escape it or we get consumed by it, often amplifying it with our thoughts. Mindfulness offers a third option—being with pain with clear, compassionate awareness.

The RAIN practice, popularized by meditation teacher Tara Brach, offers a practical framework:

- **R**ecognize the pain (name it clearly).
- **A**llow it to be there (stop fighting against it).
- **I**nvestigate with kindness (feel its qualities in body and mind).
- **N**urture yourself with compassion (hold yourself as you would a loved one in pain).

This practice doesn't eliminate pain, but it transforms our relationship to it. By creating space around pain rather than closely identifying with it, we access a dimension of ourselves that remains whole even amidst suffering. As meditation teacher Jon Kabat-Zinn notes, "You can't stop the waves, but you can learn to surf."

The Sacred Art of Surrender and Acceptance

Perhaps the most challenging and profound spiritual teaching about suffering is the practice of surrender. This doesn't mean passive resignation to injustice or preventable harm. Rather, it means releasing our resistance to what is already present. It means accepting reality before deciding how to respond to it. This surrender is not defeat—it is the beginning of authentic power.

As the Alcoholics Anonymous Serenity Prayer wisely articulates, "God, grant me the serenity to accept the things I cannot change, courage to change the things I can, and wisdom to know the difference." This simple prayer captures the essence of spiritual surrender. There are aspects of our situation we can and should change, but many others that we must simply accept. Discernment between these categories is essential wisdom.

Acceptance is surrender's close companion. While surrender relates to our will, acceptance involves embracing reality as it is, without judgment or rejection. Buddhist teacher Ajahn Chah famously held up a glass and said, "This glass is already broken." He explained that seeing the glass's impermanence while it's still whole allows us to enjoy it fully without being devastated when it inevitably breaks. Similarly, accepting our own vulnerability and mortality—not in a morbid way but with clear awareness—paradoxically enhances our capacity to live with vitality.

My own experience with acceptance came through a health crisis several years after leaving my birth nation. The diagnosis was initially devastating, and I found myself cycling through denial, anger, and despair. Only when I finally accepted the reality of my condition—neither minimizing nor catastrophizing it—could I respond effectively. This acceptance wasn't a one-time decision, but a daily practice of acknowledging what was true in each moment. The paradox: only by accepting limitations could I discover possibilities within them.

Both surrender and acceptance require tremendous courage. They ask us to face reality without the buffer of denial or the illusion of control. Yet countless spiritual practitioners across traditions testify that this courage leads to an unexpected freedom. When we stop demanding that life conform to our preferences and instead open to what is, we often discover resources, connections, and meanings previously invisible to us.

As the Zen saying goes, "The obstacle is the path." What we resist most often contains our greatest opportunity for growth.

Transcendence: Moving Beyond Self Through Suffering's Gateway

At the heart of spiritual traditions worldwide lies a paradoxical teaching: the path to liberation often leads through, not around, our greatest suffering. When navigated consciously, pain can crack open the shell of our limited identity, allowing us to experience dimensions of reality and selfhood that transcend our ordinary boundaries.

This transcendence doesn't mean escaping or denying our human experience, but expanding beyond its usual constraints. Physical pain, emotional anguish, or existential crisis, under the right conditions, can serve as gateways to this expansion. How does this happen?

First, intense suffering often shatters our normal conceptual frameworks. Our usual ways of making sense of the world may fail in the face of overwhelming pain or loss. This collapse, while initially disorienting, can clear space for direct experience beyond our mental constructs. As Zen teaches, "Great doubt, great awakening. Small doubt, small awakening. No doubt, no awakening." Our deepest questioning often precedes our most profound realizations.

Second, suffering can dissolve our sense of separation. When we suffer intensely, the carefully maintained boundaries between "self" and "other" often become more permeable. In grief, we may feel connected to all who have ever lost a loved one. In physical pain, we might develop spontaneous compassion for all beings who suffer similarly. This recognition of shared humanity is a form of transcendence—moving beyond the isolated self into wider identification.

My own experience with transcendence came unexpectedly. During a period of intense pain following personal loss, I reached a point where something surrendered within me. In that moment of complete letting go, I experienced what can only be described as grace—a profound sense of being held by something infinitely larger than my personal self. The suffering didn't disappear, but my identification with it shifted dramatically. I realized I was not only the one suffering but also the awareness within which that suffering appeared—vast, compassionate, and somehow untouched even while fully present with the pain.

Such experiences cannot be manufactured, nor should they be expected as guaranteed outcomes of suffering. They arrive as gifts, often when we've exhausted our usual strategies of control or escape. They remind us that transcendence isn't something we achieve but something we open to when our usual self-structure has been humbled by life's intensity.

Integrating Spiritual Wisdom into Daily Resilience

The spiritual dimensions of suffering we've explored are profound, but their value lies in how they inform our everyday lives. How do we translate these deep insights into practical resilience as we navigate work stress, relationship challenges, health issues, and the myriad difficulties of ordinary existence?

Integration begins with regular practice. The contemplative approaches mentioned earlier—mindfulness, prayer, meditation—build capacity that serves us when crises arrive. Just as athletes train muscles before competition, spiritual practice trains our awareness and response patterns before life tests us. Even five minutes daily of conscious breathing or present-moment awareness gradually rewires our default reactions to difficulty.

Next, integration involves applying spiritual principles to everyday challenges. When stuck in traffic, practice acceptance. When criticized at work, notice reactivity without immediately defending. When experiencing physical discomfort, bring mindful attention to sensations rather than immediate avoidance. These small moments build the neural pathways that serve us in larger crises.

Community provides another integration pathway. Spiritual wisdom isn't meant to be practiced in isolation. Whether through formal religious communities, meditation groups, support circles, or simply conversations with like-minded friends, sharing our journey multiplies its transformative power. In community, we both receive support during our dark nights and offer guidance to others from our hard-won insights.

The most profound integration happens through service to others. When we use our own suffering as motivation to ease others' pain, we participate in sacred alchemy. This doesn't mean denying or transcending our own needs, but it does mean recognizing how our wounds can become sources of connection and compassion. As theologian Henri Nouwen described, we can become "wounded healers"—those whose personal suffering becomes a source of authentic healing presence for others.

The goal isn't to reach some permanent state of enlightened perfection beyond all suffering. Rather, it's to develop a resilient, compassionate relationship with the full spectrum of human experience—including pain—informed by the wisdom these spiritual traditions offer. Just as Jack Kornfield wisely titled his book, *After the Ecstasy, the Laundry*, we must learn how to integrate spiritual experiences into everyday life and navigate the mundane with wisdom.

Pain-to-Power Exercises — Chapter 8

1. Witness Practice: For this exercise, find a quiet place where you won't be disturbed for fifteen minutes. Close your eyes and bring attention to your breath. Then recall a current challenge or pain in your life. (Start with something moderately difficult, not your deepest wound.) As you hold this situation in awareness, practice these steps:

1. Notice any physical sensations that arise (tension, heaviness, constriction) without trying to change them.
2. Observe any emotions present (sadness, fear, anger) with an attitude of allowing.
3. Witness the thoughts and stories your mind creates about this situation.
4. Ask yourself, "Who is aware of all this?" Rest in that awareness itself.

Notice if any shift occurs in your relationship to the pain when you identify with the witnessing awareness instead of the content of experience. Record any insights in a journal. With practice, this witnessing perspective can provide crucial space even amid intense suffering.

2. Sacred Meaning Inquiry: Take a piece of paper and draw a line down the middle. On the left side, describe a significant painful experience from your past. On the right side, explore what meaning or purpose has emerged from this experience, using these prompts:

- What strengths or capacities developed in me because of this challenge?
- How did this experience change my priorities or values?
- What deeper understandings about life emerged from this difficulty?
- How has this suffering connected me more authentically with others?
- What am I now able to offer others because of what I've been through?

This is not about glossing over pain or claiming that everything happens for a reason, but about recognizing how you have created meaning from difficulty. If meaning hasn't yet emerged from a recent pain, simply note "still unfolding" and trust the process.

3. Daily Transcendence Practice: For one week, commit to a daily practice of expanding beyond your normal sense of self. Choose one of these approaches (or alternate between them):

- **Compassion Expansion:** Spend five minutes each day contemplating how your personal suffering connects you with all beings who suffer similarly. With each breath, imagine your awareness expanding to include others—in your family, community, country, and eventually all beings experiencing similar challenges. Notice how this wider perspective affects your relationship to your own pain.
- **Nature Dissolution:** Spend time daily in nature (even a small park or your own backyard). Focus on a natural element—tree, sky, water—and gradually let the boundaries between yourself and this element soften. Experience yourself as part of nature rather than separate from it. Many find that this dissolution of boundaries provides perspective on personal suffering.
- **Gratitude Gateway:** Each evening, identify three moments of beauty, connection, or grace you experienced that day despite any difficulties. This practice doesn't deny suffering but places it in a larger context, allowing glimpses of transcendence within ordinary life.

Keep brief notes on how these practices affect your relationship with current challenges. Over time, this expanded perspective can become more available during difficult moments.

The diverse philosophies and scientific insights we've explored show us principles for transforming pain, but nothing illustrates these concepts more powerfully than witnessing them in action through real lives. This chapter presents remarkable individuals who have converted profound suffering into extraordinary achievement, purpose, and influence. Their stories move beyond theory to demonstrate the universal human capacity to alchemize pain into power across vastly different circumstances and challenges.

CHAPTER 9

Stories of Transformation

From Pain to Extraordinary Power

Lives Transformed Through Suffering's Crucible

In December 2008, Elon Musk stood at the precipice of total failure. His electric car company, Tesla, was hemorrhaging cash and struggling to deliver its first vehicle. SpaceX had just experienced its third consecutive rocket failure. His personal fortune, earned from the sale of PayPal years earlier, had been poured into both companies and was nearly depleted. Divorce proceedings had begun with his first wife. The global financial crisis had slammed shut any hope of raising additional funds. Depression loomed.

"I remember thinking," Musk would later recall, "the only thing I have left is my kids. At least, no matter what happens, I'll still have them."

At this darkest hour, when most would have surrendered, Musk made a fateful decision. He would bet his last remaining funds—just enough for one more rocket launch attempt and one final funding round for Tesla. It was, by any rational measure, a reckless gamble. Yet this moment of extreme adversity ultimately gave birth to two of the most revolutionary companies of our time. SpaceX's fourth launch succeeded, securing a $1.6 billion NASA contract. Days before Tesla would have gone bankrupt, last-minute funding arrived.

This pivotal moment shows how great achievement often comes as a result of suffering. In the dark days after fleeing my motherland, I, too, wondered if my pain would ever become something meaningful. The loss of my homeland, my career, and my daily connection with loved ones all felt like an open wound that might never heal. During this period, I found myself drawn to stories of others who had faced devastating circumstances and somehow came out the other side better. Their journeys inspired me that my pain *could* transform me if I engaged with it rather than merely endured it.

In this chapter, we'll explore how remarkable individuals have transformed profound suffering into extraordinary achievement, purpose, and strength. From Musk's corporate near-death experience to Malala Yousafzai's response to violence, from Viktor Frankl's concentration camp insights to Oprah Winfrey's journey from abuse to influence—these stories reveal the universal human capacity to alchemize pain into power.

Elon Musk: Fire-Forged Innovation

Early Hardships: The Crucible of Youth

Long before Elon Musk became a household name, his capacity for enduring and learning from suffering was being forged in childhood. Born in Pretoria, South Africa, in 1971, Musk's early years contained significant challenges that would shape his resilience and drive.

By his own account, Musk endured severe bullying in school. In one particularly brutal incident, a group of boys threw him down a flight of concrete stairs and then beat him unconscious, requiring hospitalization. This wasn't an isolated event—Musk described being "almost beaten to death" on multiple occasions. For a sensitive, highly intelligent child, this physical and social torment created deep suffering.

Home life presented its own difficulties. After his parents divorced when he was nine, Musk eventually chose to live with his father—a decision he would later describe as a mistake. In interviews, he has characterized his father as "a terrible human being" and described his childhood as "painful and isolated."

114

These early experiences could have broken many children, but for Musk, they became formative. He retreated into books and computers, developing a rich inner world and technical skills that would later serve him well. The isolation drove him to become self-reliant. The bullying instilled a certain indifference to social rejection and criticism that would later enable him to pursue wildly unconventional ideas in the face of skepticism.

At age seventeen, Musk made another pivotal choice born from difficulty: he left South Africa partly to avoid mandatory military service under the apartheid regime. Arriving alone in Canada with minimal resources, he sometimes lived on just $1 per day, subsisting on hot dogs and oranges. He took odd jobs, including cleaning boilers at a lumber mill—dangerous work requiring him to crawl through confined spaces wearing a hazmat suit in 120-degree heat.

These early hardships were not incidental to Musk's later success—they were instrumental. They developed his capacity to endure discomfort, take risks, and operate outside conventional comfort zones. As he would later reflect: "When something is important enough, you do it even if the odds are not in your favor."

Betting Everything: Near-Bankruptcies and Failed Launches

If childhood formed Musk's capacity for enduring pain, his entrepreneurial journey repeatedly tested that capacity to its limits. His approach to business risk has consistently involved placing himself at the edge of financial and emotional disaster—and sometimes stepping over that edge.

After selling his first company, Zip2, for $307 million in 1999, Musk co-founded the online payment system that would eventually become PayPal. Though this venture ultimately succeeded, the path was not without difficulty. In fact, Musk was ousted as CEO while on honeymoon—the first of several leadership challenges he would face throughout his career. Nevertheless, when eBay acquired PayPal in 2002, Musk netted approximately $180 million.

At this point, most people would have settled into comfortable wealth, but Musk did the opposite. He invested nearly all his fortune into two highly improbable ventures: SpaceX and Tesla. Both companies faced problems that had defeated numerous predecessors, from the extraordinary technical challenges of private space flight to the manufacturing and market complexities of electric vehicles.

The years 2007–2008 brought Musk to what he has called the most difficult period of his life. Tesla's first vehicle, the Roadster, faced severe production delays and cost overruns. SpaceX had achieved three consecutive rocket launch failures. The financial crisis had dried up potential investment exactly when both companies desperately needed capital. Further, Musk was going through a divorce. His entire fortune had been invested in his companies, and they were both failing simultaneously.

This convergence of personal and professional crises would have broken many people, and Musk later revealed that he suffered from something "close to a nervous breakdown" during this time. Yet instead of retreating, he doubled down. He borrowed money for rent, secured a high-interest loan from a friend to keep Tesla afloat, and prepared for a fourth rocket launch that represented SpaceX's final chance.

"I could either keep the money—then the companies would definitely die—or invest the money, and maybe the companies would die," Musk explained. "If I held onto the money, then I'd feel bad about the companies dying. I'd rather the companies would die than I would feel bad about it."

This willingness to risk everything—to potentially lose all financial security—reveals something crucial about Musk's relationship with adversity. He accepted the possibility of total failure rather than living with the certainty of regret. By facing his worst fears directly, he paradoxically freed himself to act with full commitment.

The fourth Falcon 1 rocket launch succeeded in September 2008, becoming the first privately developed liquid-fuel rocket to reach orbit. Two months later, with Tesla literally hours from bankruptcy, the company secured a critical investment round. Both companies survived by the narrowest of margins.

What's remarkable isn't just that Musk's companies survived these crises, but how these near-death experiences shaped their development. The constant pressure of potential failure drove extraordinary innovation. Tesla pioneered new approaches to manufacturing, battery technology, and software integration

THE POWER OF PAIN

precisely because conventional approaches wouldn't work fast enough to save the company. SpaceX developed its revolutionary reusable rocket technology partly because cost reduction was existential, not merely desirable.

Innovation Borne of Necessity: How Crisis Shaped Revolutionary Companies

A fascinating aspect of Musk's relationship with adversity is how directly his companies' innovations have emerged from periods of crisis. Far from being incidental to his achievements, his most revolutionary ideas were repeatedly forged during times of duress.

SpaceX's development of reusable rockets provides a compelling example. The company was founded with the ambitious goal of making humanity multiplanetary, but early failures threatened its existence. After three consecutive launch failures nearly bankrupted the company in 2008, SpaceX faced an existential reality: conventional aerospace approaches were too expensive to be commercially viable at their scale.

This crisis forced a radical rethinking that established players, comfortable in their government contracts, had no incentive to attempt. SpaceX engineers, driven by necessity, pioneered technologies to recover and reuse rocket boosters—something the aerospace industry had deemed impractical or impossible. After multiple dramatic failures (including rockets exploding during landing attempts), SpaceX achieved what had never been done before: landing an orbital-class rocket booster for reuse.

This innovation, born directly from financial and technical adversity, reduced launch costs by approximately 80 percent and revolutionized the economics of space access. Had SpaceX been more comfortable—had it not faced the pain of near-bankruptcy and technical failure—it might never have pushed for such a transformative approach.

Tesla's journey shows a similar pattern. During the company's 2008 financial crisis, Musk made the painful decision to lay off about 25 percent of Tesla's workforce and negotiate with investors from a position of extreme weakness. This crisis forced a fundamental reassessment of the company's approach. Rather than continuing with their original business plan to be a niche sports car manufacturer, Tesla pivoted toward becoming a mass-market automaker with an integrated energy business.

This pivot, born from financial desperation, ultimately led to Tesla's development of technologies that traditional automakers had neglected, from advanced battery systems to over-the-air software updates. The suffering of that near-death experience became the catalyst for innovations that later defined the company's competitive advantage.

Musk has repeatedly emphasized that pain and sacrifice are inseparable from meaningful achievement: "Starting a company is like eating glass and staring into the abyss." This vivid metaphor captures both the physical discomfort and psychological terror of entrepreneurship at his level. Yet he has consistently chosen this difficult path, knowing that transformative innovation requires embracing rather than avoiding pain.

The Musk Method: Practical Lessons in Embracing Difficulty

Beyond inspiration, Musk's approach to adversity offers practical principles we can apply to our own challenges—regardless of whether we're building rockets or simply navigating personal difficulties. His methodology for transforming pain into progress contains transferable insights for anyone seeking to accomplish difficult goals.

1. **First-principles thinking:** When facing seemingly insurmountable problems, Musk employs what he calls "first-principles thinking"— breaking challenges down to their fundamental truths rather than reasoning by analogy or convention. This approach proved crucial during SpaceX's early days when the cost of existing rockets threatened the company's viability.

Rather than accepting conventional aerospace wisdom, Musk asked, "What are rockets made of? Aerospace-grade aluminum alloys, plus some titanium, copper, and carbon fiber. And what is the value of those materials on the commodity market? It turned out the materials cost of a rocket was around 2 percent of the typical price."

This analysis revealed that the problem wasn't fundamental physics or material costs but rather industry practices and assumptions. By questioning these assumptions, SpaceX found a path to dramatically lower launch costs.

2. **Calculated risk and fallback planning:** Contrary to his public image as a reckless risk-taker, Musk's approach involves careful calculation of both risk and contingency. When deciding whether to invest his last remaining funds in Tesla and SpaceX during their 2008 crisis, he didn't simply hope for the best; he developed specific fallback plans.

"Even if the companies fail," he reasoned, "I know I can always get a job and make enough money to pay the rent. My kids will never go hungry. I figured I could be in a pretty bad situation but still afford food to eat."

This pragmatic assessment—identifying the true worst case and confirming it was survivable—enabled him to take risks that seemed reckless to outside observers but were actually carefully considered.

3. **Normalizing difficulty:** Perhaps most fundamentally, Musk has normalized difficulty as an expected part of meaningful achievement. "If you're trying to create a company," he has said, "it's like baking a cake. You have to have all the ingredients in the right proportion." When asked what those ingredients are, he replied, "You have to have a very high pain threshold."

This normalization—the explicit expectation that significant achievement requires significant pain—creates psychological readiness for the inevitable challenges of ambitious work. Rather than being surprised or demoralized by difficulty, Musk and his teams expect and prepare for it.

We can apply these principles by consciously shifting our mental models around pain and achievement. When difficulties arise, rather than asking, "Why is this so hard?" (implying something is wrong), we might ask, "How can I best navigate this expected challenge?" This reframing transforms our thinking: we stop seeing adversity as a sign of failure and rather see it as an anticipated part of the journey.

Nelson Mandela: From Prisoner to President – Forgiveness as Freedom

Nelson Mandela spent twenty-seven years in prison under South Africa's apartheid regime, much of it in a tiny cell on Robben Island, where he performed hard labor. He was cut off from his family and the normal course of life from age forty-four to seventy-one. It's hard to fathom losing so many years, yet Mandela emerged from prison without bitterness. Instead, he famously preached reconciliation and forgiveness, leading South Africa into a peaceful transition to democracy as its first Black president.

Mandela's story is a testament to the power of purpose and perspective. In prison, he kept his mind active and spirits up by secretly writing, educating younger inmates, and maintaining the mindset that he was a freedom fighter, not a victim. His long-term vision of a free and equal South Africa gave meaning to his daily suffering. He later said, "As I walked out the door toward the gate that would lead to my freedom, I knew if I didn't leave my bitterness and hatred behind, I'd still be in prison."

This perspective resonated deeply with me during my early years in America. Though my circumstances were incomparably less harsh than Mandela's imprisonment, I, too, faced the challenge of maintaining purpose despite forced separation from my country. There were days when bitterness threatened to consume me—anger at the regime that had driven me out, resentment toward those who didn't understand my struggle, and even jealousy toward Americans who took their freedom for granted. Mandela's example reminded me that hanging onto these feelings would only create a prison of my own making, regardless of my physical freedom.

By forgiving his captors and oppressors, Mandela not only liberated his country but also freed himself from the destructive effects of hatred. He exemplified that resilience can mean turning pain into wisdom and compassion. The Truth and Reconciliation Commission he supported asked victims and perpetrators of apartheid-era violence to come forward and speak the truth in exchange (in some cases) for amnesty. It was a bold, painful process for the nation, but ultimately a healing one.

The lesson we can learn from Mandela's triumph is that holding onto purpose and practicing forgiveness can transform even lifelong suffering into an influence that changes the world.

Malala Yousafzai: The Girl Who Stood Up – Courage and Voice

Malala Yousafzai was only fifteen years old when the Taliban boarded her school bus in Pakistan, called out her name, and shot her in the head for her outspoken advocacy of girls' education. Remarkably, Malala survived the assassination attempt after intensive medical care in the UK. Even more remarkable was what she did with her second chance at life. Instead of being silenced by fear, Malala's voice grew louder. On her sixteenth birthday—just nine months after the shooting—she stood before the United Nations and delivered a historic speech, declaring, "They thought that the bullets would silence us, but they failed. . . . Weakness, fear, and hopelessness died. Strength, power, and courage were born."

Malala's courage became a touchstone for me during my darkest periods of doubt. After DolarToday gained recognition, threats toward me, as well as my family, intensified. I found myself at a crossroads, weighing the comfort of silence against the call to continue speaking the truth. The quiet life in America beckoned—a chance to build something personal, protected, far from the dangers of activism.

However, in my moments of wavering, Malala's story would resurface in my thoughts. This young girl had stared down the barrel of extremism and paid with her blood for the simple act of seeking education, yet she had emerged with a stronger voice than before. Her resilience stripped away my excuses: if a teenager could face assassins' bullets and still rise to speak for what she believed in, how could I justify retreating from lesser threats? Her example didn't erase my fear, but it provided the perspective I needed to move through it. Each time I considered stepping back from our mission, I would remember the hospital bed where she continued her fight—and find the resolve to continue mine.

Malala's story is one of incredible bravery and clarity of purpose in the face of extreme trauma. She turned an act of violence meant to instill terror into a rallying cry heard around the world. At seventeen, she became the youngest Nobel Peace Prize laureate, recognized for her unwavering struggle for girls' right to education.

What allowed Malala to transform this trauma into global advocacy? First, her belief in her cause was unshakable. Even as she recovered, she understood that the attack wasn't just on her but on every girl who wants to learn. That knowledge fueled her determination rather than her fear. Second, Malala embraced compassion over hatred. In her UN speech, she even extended forgiveness, saying she didn't wish revenge on the Taliban militant who shot her. Instead, she spoke about education for the sons and daughters of extremists too.

From Malala we learn that standing up for one's values and turning personal trauma into a voice for others can not only heal one's own wounds but inspire millions. Malala shows that courage and education are stronger than fear and ignorance.

Viktor Frankl: Finding Meaning in the Camps – Purpose in Darkness

We've discussed Viktor Frankl's ideas; now a bit on his story. Frankl was a successful young neurologist and psychiatrist in Vienna when World War II erupted. Because he was Jewish, he and his family were deported to Nazi concentration camps. He endured indescribable horrors in Auschwitz and other camps. His father, mother, brother, and pregnant wife all perished. In these depths of suffering, Frankl observed something profound (as mentioned earlier): that those prisoners who found a meaning for their suffering were more likely to survive.

During my darkest days of cultural disorientation and homesickness, I turned to Frankl's writings repeatedly. If he could find meaning in the concentration camps—the most extreme human suffering imaginable—surely I could find purpose in my exile. His insights helped me reframe my journey: I wasn't just a displaced person; I was a witness to Venezuela's struggle, a voice for those who couldn't speak freely, and eventually a bridge between cultures. This meaning-making transformed my experience from mere loss into a purposeful transition.

Frankl survived three years in the camps. During that time, in addition to holding on to the love for his wife (not knowing her fate until after the war), he imagined himself in the future lecturing to students about the psychology of the concentration camp, helping them understand that there can be meaning in suffering. This visualization gave him a sense of purpose—he felt he must survive to deliver this message to the world. Indeed, after liberation, he did exactly that, writing *Man's Search for Meaning* in just nine days. The book has since helped millions find hope in despair.

Frankl's personal triumph was that he did not let the Holocaust make him cynical or hateful. Instead, he validated the potential in humans to remain humane. He later founded logotherapy, helping patients find meaning in their own lives. The motto he often quoted from Nietzsche is, "He who has a why to live can bear almost any how."

From Frankl we learn that when we are helpless to change our circumstances, we retain the freedom to choose our attitude. By finding meaning—whether in love, faith, hope, or duty—we can endure and transform suffering into a source of strength.

Frida Kahlo: Art from Pain – Creating Beauty from Brokenness

Frida Kahlo, the renowned Mexican painter, is an icon of artistic genius forged through pain. As a child, she survived polio, which left one leg thinner and weaker. At eighteen, she was in a catastrophic bus accident: a metal handrail impaled her abdomen and pelvis, and her spine and many bones were fractured. She was in a full-body cast and endured over thirty surgeries throughout her life. Chronic pain and medical complications became her constant companions. She also longed for children but suffered multiple miscarriages, likely due to the accident injuries.

Confined to bed for long periods, Kahlo began to paint, using a special easel that allowed her to paint lying down. She famously said, "I paint self-portraits because I am so often alone, because I am the subject I know best." Her paintings are vibrant, raw, and often surreal depictions of her physical and emotional agony— yet they are also celebrated for their beauty, color, and strength. She turned her pain into art that resonates universally.

Frida also embraced her identity and uniqueness fiercely. She defied gender norms and embraced her Mexican indigenous culture in her style. Despite being physically limited at times, she lived boldly—engaging in politics, having passionate relationships, and turning every aspect of her life into a form of creative expression.

As a Latin American immigrant myself, I found particular resonance with Kahlo's work. Her paintings blend personal pain with cultural identity, showing how our roots sustain us even amid suffering. During periods when I felt caught between worlds—no longer fully connected to my heritage but not yet fully American— Kahlo's ability to create from this cultural borderland inspired me. Her fearless self-expression encouraged me to incorporate my roots and cultural identity into my new life rather than trying to erase them in pursuit of assimilation.

From Kahlo we learn that art and creativity can be a lifeline in pain. By expressing our pain through art, whether it be painting, drawing, writing, dancing, or otherwise, we can transform it into something meaningful and even beautiful. Our scars can become our art, our message.

Stephen Hawking: A Mind Beyond Limitations

Stephen Hawking was one of the most brilliant theoretical physicists of our time, famous for his work on black holes and the origins of the universe. But equally inspiring is the fact that he did this groundbreaking work while suffering from a debilitating illness. At twenty-one, Hawking was diagnosed with ALS (amyotrophic lateral sclerosis), a motor neuron disease. Doctors gave him about two years to live. Yet Hawking defied every prognosis, living to the age of seventy-six and contributing to science for decades, even after he lost the ability to walk, move almost any muscles, and eventually even speak without a computerized voice.

When I struggled with the limitations that come with being an immigrant—the language barriers, credential recognition issues, and cultural adjustments—I sometimes fell into self-pity. Why was everything so much harder for me than for native-born Americans? Hawking's story provided a powerful perspective shift. Here was a man whose physical limitations dwarfed my challenges, yet he focused relentlessly on what he could do rather than what he couldn't. If he could explore the cosmos from a wheelchair, surely I could build a new life despite my own obstacles.

How did Hawking turn the crushing news of a terminal illness into a lifetime of achievement? He often cited that initially, he fell into depression after diagnosis, seeing no point in finishing his PhD. But when his health stabilized somewhat and he realized he might not die as quickly as predicted, he had a change of perspective. He said, "My expectations were reduced to zero when I was twenty-one. Everything since then has been a bonus."

Hawking's story is about adaptation and attitude. As his physical abilities diminished, he adapted with technology (like his speech synthesizer) and with an increasing reliance on collaborators and caretakers. But notably, Hawking retained a sense of humor and curiosity about life. He once said, "However difficult life may seem, there is always something you can do and succeed at."

Hawking teaches us to embrace our abilities, however limited the world might think they are, and keep our sense of wonder. A change in perspective can make life's "bonus" years incredibly rich and impactful, even under extreme constraints.

Harriet Tubman: The Moses of Her People – Perseverance and Purpose

Harriet Tubman was born into slavery in the United States around 1822. Her life was filled with brutal pain from the start. As a young girl, she was whipped and beaten by masters. She also suffered a traumatic head injury as a teenager when an overseer threw a heavy metal weight intending to hit another slave and struck Harriet instead. The injury caused her lifelong severe headaches, seizures, and narcoleptic episodes. Despite this, Harriet Tubman possessed extraordinary determination.

Tubman's story holds special significance for me because of her repeated returns to danger. After escaping slavery herself, she could have settled safely in the North, yet she chose to go back—again and again—risking her life to guide others to freedom. In my own small way, I've faced this tension: the safety of focusing solely on my American life versus the call to remain engaged with Venezuela's struggle, which brings both emotional pain and some risk. Tubman's courage in returning to danger for a larger purpose has been a North Star when I've questioned whether continued activism is worth the cost.

In her twenties, Harriet escaped from slavery, making the dangerous journey north to freedom via the Underground Railroad (a secret network of safe houses). But her own freedom wasn't enough; she felt compelled to return, again and again, to slave-holding states to lead others out. Over about a decade, she undertook some thirteen missions and rescued approximately seventy enslaved people, including family and friends, guiding them to freedom. She never lost a single passenger.

Harriet's resilience came from a deep spiritual faith and sense of mission. She believed God was guiding and protecting her. She also displayed incredible ingenuity and toughness—carrying a gun both to fend off pursuers and to encourage any of her frightened escapees who might waver. Later, during the Civil War, Tubman served as a scout and spy for the Union Army, even leading an armed expedition that liberated seven hundred slaves.

The lesson we learn from Tubman is that a purpose larger than us can give us the strength to overcome and dare unimaginable feats. When pain is transmuted into compassion and courage, it can literally change the course of history.

Oprah Winfrey: From Abuse to Influence – Healing and Empowerment

Oprah Winfrey is a household name, synonymous with success and empathy as a media giant, but her beginnings were filled with hardship and trauma. Born to a teenage single mother in Mississippi, she grew up in poverty. As a child, Oprah faced repeated sexual abuse from relatives and family friends. She has spoken openly about how this abuse and the lack of stable support led her to rebel and run away; she even became pregnant at fourteen. She lost the baby shortly after birth—a tragedy that could have derailed her life entirely.

When I reflect on my journey from my homeland to the United States, I see parallels with Oprah's transformation—not in the specific hardships we faced, but in the process of reinvention. Like her, I had to reimagine who I could be in a new context. When my previous identity as a military lieutenant and a respected citizen was stripped away, I had to rebuild from the foundation. Oprah's ability to redefine herself without denying her past inspired me to integrate my cultural experiences into my American identity rather than trying to erase them.

Oprah's story is one of remarkable turnaround. She found solace and strength in education and eventually in speaking—winning oratory contests and excelling in drama, which led to a career in broadcasting. By nineteen, she was co-anchoring the local evening news. Over the years, her natural warmth and ability to connect with people propelled her to host her own talk show in Chicago, which later became the nationally syndicated *Oprah Winfrey Show*, the highest-rated talk show in history for twenty-five years.

Oprah transformed her painful past into an ability to empathize deeply with others' pain. On her show, she created a space where taboo topics—like sexual abuse, addiction, and trauma—could be discussed openly and compassionately. This was revolutionary in a time when such issues were often buried in shame. Survivors saw in her a living example that you can overcome and even thrive, and she often said sharing our stories is part of healing.

The lesson we learn from Oprah is that our deepest pain can become a platform for our greatest impact. By healing herself, pursuing her potential, and openly helping others heal, Oprah turned personal trauma into a worldwide source of empowerment.

My Journey: From Exile to Purpose – A Personal Testimony

While the stories above have inspired and guided me, my own journey of transformation deserves a place in this chapter as well. Like those whose lives we've explored, I, too, have experienced how pain can become a catalyst for growth, meaning, and unexpected strength.

In 2005, as my country descended deeper into authoritarianism under the regime of Hugo Chávez, I faced an agonizing decision. As a former military lieutenant who had spoken out against government corruption, I found myself increasingly at risk. The breaking point came when a bomb exploded under my car—a clear message that my voice was considered dangerous enough to silence permanently. By some miracle, I wasn't in the vehicle at that moment.

The decision to leave was excruciating. I had to bid farewell to a hard-earned career, beloved family and friends, and the warm embrace of home—the culture, language, and traditions that defined my identity. Yet, in the midst of this overwhelming pain, I understood that true courage lay in choosing change over stagnation. With nothing but determination, I stepped into the unknown, arriving in the United States with limited funds and minimal English but an unyielding desire to fight for freedom.

In the early years of immigration, I faced daily battles—cultural barriers, language challenges, financial hardships, and the raw emotional pain of displacement. I worked jobs far below my previous status, struggled to communicate my most basic needs, and spent many nights wondering if I had made the right choice. The loss of professional identity was particularly painful; in Venezuela, I had been respected for my mind and leadership, but in America, I was initially valued only for my hands—for the physical labor I could perform.

Yet even in this darkness, seeds of transformation were beginning to grow. I recognized that by leaving, I was not simply seeking a new beginning for myself; I was positioning myself to challenge an oppressive regime from afar. The government's subsequent lawsuit against DolarToday in the United States and the escalation of threats to my family confirmed that our work was making a difference—enough to make powerful people uncomfortable. What had begun as a desperate flight from danger was evolving into something purposeful. Each threat, each attempt to silence us, only illuminated more clearly why continuing our mission mattered. From the safety of exile, I could speak truths that would be fatal to voice from within my country's borders. My pain and loss weren't just burdens to bear—they were becoming the very foundation of a new identity: not just as a refugee who had fled, but as an activist who could fight.

What I've learned through my journey—and what connects it to the other stories in this chapter—is that transformation happens when we refuse to be defined solely by our suffering. By embracing my role as a witness and advocate, by finding community among fellow expatriates from my native land in exile, by using education as a ladder to rebuild my professional life, and by maintaining a vision of freedom that transcends my personal circumstances, I've been able to convert the pain of displacement into purposeful action.

The lesson from my experiences is that sometimes leaving is itself an act of courage. By transforming the pain of displacement into advocacy, community-building, and personal reinvention, we can honor our roots while growing new branches that reach toward light.

Common Threads: The Tapestry of Human Resilience

As we reflect on the stories of Musk, Mandela, Malala, Frankl, Kahlo, Hawking, Tubman, Oprah, and myself, we can see the depths of human resilience. While no two journeys are the same, there are some commonalities in our stories:

1. **Finding meaning beyond the self:** Each person connected their suffering to something larger—a cause, an art form, a community in need, a scientific pursuit, or a spiritual understanding. This connection transformed their pain from a purely private burden into something with purpose and dignity.

2. **Refusing victim identity:** While acknowledging real victimization or misfortune, none of these individuals defined themselves primarily as victims. They recognized what was done to them or what circumstance they faced, but they didn't allow that recognition to become their core identity.

3. **Adapting rather than surrendering:** Each faced limitations that could have ended their pursuits, but they found creative ways to adapt. Hawking developed communication systems when he could no longer speak, Kahlo painted from her bed when she couldn't stand, and I found new ways to continue my education despite language barriers.

4. **Leveraging community:** None of these journeys happened in isolation. Each person had key relationships, communities, or supporters who provided practical help, emotional sustenance, or simply a witness to their struggle.

5. **Maintaining hope without denying reality:** Perhaps most striking is how each balanced clear-eyed recognition of painful reality with genuine hope. They neither minimized their suffering through toxic positivity nor surrendered to cynicism or despair.

You don't have to be famous to do this. Every day, people around us are quietly turning their hardships into something meaningful—raising children with love despite their own loveless childhoods, starting social initiatives after surviving tragedy, or simply becoming kinder and wiser people through their struggles. In your own life, you are the hero of your story. You have the capacity for the same resilience these figures showed.

These patterns provide a practical framework for approaching our own suffering. By connecting our pain to something beyond ourselves, refusing to be defined primarily as victims, adapting creatively to limitations, leveraging supportive communities, and balancing clear-eyed realism with genuine hope, we, too, can become empowered through our pain. Their stories aren't meant to intimidate, but to illuminate the path that is available to each of us, regardless of our specific circumstances or our sphere of influence.

Pain-to-Power Exercises – Chapter 9

1. Personal Hero Reflection: Among the stories in this chapter (or maybe another who inspires you), choose one person who resonates most with you. Write down what about their story inspires you and what qualities or actions they took that you'd like to emulate. Then, identify a challenge in your own life and ask, "What would [Hero] do or think in this situation?" This isn't to compare unfairly, but to remind yourself that you can channel those same qualities. For example, "Malala showed fearless dedication to education; I can channel a bit of that courage to go back to school as an adult," or, "Hawking kept creating despite loss; I won't let my setbacks stop me from my art." This exercise helps you translate abstract inspiration into concrete perspective shifts that will help you overcome challenges.

2. Write Your Triumph Story: Try writing a short narrative of your own life, focusing on a challenge you overcame. Frame it like one of these case studies, highlighting how you turned pain into strength. Use third person if it helps ("She had faced . . . but she persevered . . ."). This can give you a fresh, empowering perspective on your journey and reaffirm the tools you used. If you feel you're still in the middle of the story and haven't fully triumphed yet, write it as if it were a story in progress—identify the turning points that are beginning to emerge. This narrative exercise helps you recognize yourself as the hero of your own journey rather than the victim, reinforcing your agency and resilience.

3. First-Principles Challenge: Apply Elon Musk's first-principles thinking to a personal or professional obstacle you're facing. Instead of accepting conventional wisdom about your challenge, break it down to its fundamental elements. Ask, "What is the core problem? What are the essential components? What assumptions am I making that might be limiting my options?" This mental model can help you discover innovative approaches to difficulties that seem insurmountable when viewed through conventional frameworks. By questioning basic assumptions, you might find creative solutions that others miss, just as Musk did with his breakthrough innovations in space travel and electric vehicles.

The diverse journeys we've explored in this chapter demonstrate the universal human capacity to transform suffering into strength. In the next chapter, we'll examine how this transformation occurs not just in individuals but within organizations and communities. We'll discover how effective leaders convert collective challenges into innovation, cohesion, and sustainable resilience.

CHAPTER 10

The Leadership Forge

Becoming a Leader Through Your Pain

Transforming Personal Suffering into Leadership for Others

When COVID-19 hit, Elena, a Venezuelan immigrant in my community, faced a crisis that mirrored her previous life upheavals. With three children suddenly home from school and her housekeeping jobs vanishing overnight, she could have collapsed under the pressure. Yet through this dire challenge, Elena demonstrated extraordinary leadership—not just for her family, but for our entire immigrant community.

Her leadership emerged not from a formal position but through authentic vulnerability and purposeful action. In a video call with other Venezuelan families, she acknowledged the gravity of their shared situation, her voice breaking with emotion: "This is hard for all of us, but we've survived worse, and we'll find a way through this together." Within days, she had organized a mutual aid network—families sharing childcare, pooling food resources, and connecting those with technology skills to elders needing assistance.

This moment—painful, authentic, and ultimately galvanizing—exemplifies how leadership is forged during hardship. Elena, who had previously considered herself "just a mom trying to get by," demonstrated that true leadership isn't about avoiding pain but about transforming it into connection, clarity, and collective purpose. Her vulnerability became strength; her honesty became trust; her willingness to share the burden of difficult circumstances became community resilience.

From Personal Pain to Leadership Capacity

In previous chapters, we explored how individuals can transform personal suffering into inner strength. Now we turn to how this transformation extends beyond our personal growth to influence others—how our pain, when consciously engaged, can develop leadership capacities that impact families, friendships, communities, and even movements for change. When we step into leadership roles— whether as parents, friends, community volunteers, or advocates—we become responsible not just for our own response to adversity but for how we guide others through challenges.

This chapter explores how adversity serves as a forge—an intense heat source that, when properly applied, doesn't destroy but strengthens and shapes both the emerging leader and those they influence. We'll examine how failure becomes valuable feedback, personal crises catalyze wisdom, and the emotional labor of processing our own suffering creates sustainable strength that benefits others. The examples here span family relationships, friendships, community involvement, and social change, demonstrating that these principles apply wherever humans connect for collective purpose.

The Crucible Experience: How Pain Creates Authentic Leaders

Leadership often emerges from what researchers Warren Bennis and Robert Thomas call "crucible experiences"—transformative ordeals that test, challenge, and ultimately forge a person's leadership identity and capacity. These experiences are painful by definition—they push us beyond our comfort zones, confront us with failure, and force us to question our assumptions and values. Yet from these crucibles emerge leaders with deeper authenticity, greater resilience, and clearer purpose.

Consider Richard, a father in our expatriate community who lost his six-figure corporate job during an economic downturn. His identity had been deeply tied to his professional success and provider role. The months of unemployment and financial strain created a crisis not just of finances but of his fundamental self-concept.

"I went from being the person everyone came to for advice to not even knowing how to define myself," Richard told me. Yet through this painful process, he developed leadership qualities that had never emerged in his executive role. As he confronted his own vulnerability and redefined his worth beyond professional accomplishment, he became a profoundly different kind of father to his teenage children.

"Before my crisis, I led through certainty—having the answers, controlling outcomes," he explained. "Now I lead through vulnerability—asking questions, acknowledging when I don't know, and showing my kids how to navigate uncertainty rather than pretending it doesn't exist." This transformation made him a more effective guide through his children's adolescent struggles precisely because he had engaged deeply with his own pain rather than hiding it.

Similarly, Maria found unexpected leadership capacity through her journey with chronic illness. Initially devastated by her diagnosis and the limitations it imposed, she eventually founded a support group for others facing similar health challenges. "I never saw myself as a leader," she reflected. "But my pain gave me perspective that others needed. I could say, 'I know how dark this feels right now, and here's how I found my way toward light.'" Her leadership emerged not despite her suffering but through it—her continued health struggles gave her authenticity and insight that someone without that experience simply couldn't offer.

What transforms these painful experiences into leadership assets rather than liabilities? Research suggests several key factors:

Meaning-making: People who develop leadership through suffering typically engage in deliberate reflection, extracting lessons and finding meaning in their pain. They don't just endure difficulties; they interpret them. When James lost his partner to cancer, the grief was overwhelming. But through journaling and eventually joining a grief support group, he began to articulate how this loss was changing his perspective on what matters. This meaning-making process eventually led him to train as a hospice volunteer, where his hard-won wisdom now serves families facing similar losses.

Identity evolution: Crucible experiences force potential leaders to examine and often redefine their sense of self. When Sophia experienced pregnancy loss, her identity as a future mother was shattered. The process of rebuilding her sense of self included confronting societal silence around miscarriage. "I had to find new language for who I was—not just someone who had lost a baby, but someone who could help others feeling isolated in their grief." Her evolved identity eventually led her to create an online community where women share their reproductive loss stories, breaking the isolation that compounds such grief.

Values clarification: Pain often reveals what truly matters. Leaders emerge from crucibles with clearer values and stronger convictions. Carlos, who survived a near-fatal car accident, describes how his priorities crystallized during recovery: "Before, I was climbing the ladder, chasing status. After facing mortality, I couldn't pretend those things mattered to me anymore." This clarity eventually transformed his role in his extended family, where he became the person who consistently reminded everyone to prioritize relationships over achievements during family conflicts.

Adaptive capacity: Perhaps most importantly, crucibles develop what psychologists call "adaptive capacity"—the ability to respond flexibly to changing circumstances while maintaining core purpose. Leaders with high adaptive capacity neither break under pressure nor remain rigidly attached to failing approaches. They find the balance between consistency and change. Latisha demonstrated this when her carefully planned community garden project faced unexpected soil contamination issues. Rather than abandoning the project or stubbornly pushing forward with the original plan, she pivoted to container gardening while maintaining the core purpose of bringing neighbors together around food production.

These transformative benefits don't emerge automatically from suffering. Many people experience adversity without developing leadership strength. The crucial difference lies in how potential leaders engage with their pain—whether they approach it with curiosity rather than avoidance, whether they seek meaning rather than mere escape, and whether they integrate rather than compartmentalize the experience.

From Failure to Wisdom: The Journey to Earned Insight

The path to wisdom often runs directly through the territory of failure. Our most profound insights frequently emerge not from our successes but from our mistakes, disappointments, and outright failures. This pattern appears consistently in the development of leaders across contexts—from parents whose rigid approaches with their first child evolve into more nuanced guidance for younger siblings, to community organizers whose failed initial campaigns teach invaluable lessons about effective mobilization.

Amara's story exemplifies this transformation of failure into wisdom. After immigrating from Nigeria, she was determined to maintain her children's connection to their cultural heritage. Her initial approach was rigid—demanding perfect adherence to traditional practices and language at home. The result was growing resentment and resistance from her American-raised teenagers.

"I was failing as a cultural bridge-builder, the role I most wanted to succeed in," Amara told me. "My children were pulling away not just from our traditions but from me." This painful failure forced her to reflect deeply on what cultural transmission truly required. The wisdom that emerged—that connection must precede content, that cultural identity lives in relationship more than rules—transformed her approach. She began hosting Nigerian cooking sessions where English and Yoruba flowed together naturally, inviting her children's friends to join, and sharing stories about her own childhood struggles with cultural expectations.

"The failure was necessary," she now recognizes. "Without it, I would have continued imposing rather than inviting." Today, Amara's home has become a cultural hub for Nigerian families in her community, and she mentors other immigrant parents through the complex journey of raising bicultural children. The wisdom she shares was earned through painful failure rather than easy success.

The neurological basis for this transformation lies in how we process failure. When we perceive failure as identity defining ("I am a failure"), it activates threat responses in the brain—increasing stress hormones, narrowing attention, and inhibiting learning. But when reframed as information ("That approach failed; what can I learn?"), failure activates curiosity circuits that enhance creativity and adaptation. This distinction is not merely semantic—it fundamentally alters our neurological response to painful outcomes.

Psychologist Carol Dweck describes this as the difference between a "fixed mindset" and a "growth mindset." In a fixed mindset, failure represents a judgment on one's inherent abilities. In a growth mindset, failure represents valuable information about what doesn't work—a necessary step toward discovering what does. Leaders who develop wisdom through failure typically demonstrate this growth orientation, approaching disappointments with questions rather than conclusions.

This perspective transforms pain from something to be avoided into a necessary investment in wisdom—a cost of learning rather than evidence of incompetence. It explains why many family traditions include "passing down" hard-won wisdom through stories of mistakes and their consequences. These narratives serve as vicarious learning opportunities, allowing others to benefit from the narrator's painful experiences without having to repeat them.

The journey from failure to wisdom typically follows several stages:

- **Initial shock and disappointment:** The acute pain of falling short, being rejected, or watching a cherished plan collapse. Michael experienced this when his carefully planned intervention for his brother's addiction backfired, deepening family divisions rather than promoting healing.

- **Reflection and reframing:** The deliberate process of examining what happened with an orientation toward learning rather than blame. For Michael, this involved painful soul-searching about his motivations, consulting addiction professionals, and eventually recognizing how his approach had prioritized his need for control over his brother's need for dignity.
- **Integration and application:** The development of new approaches informed by the failure experience. Michael eventually became an effective support for other families navigating addiction, his approach now characterized by humility, patience, and respect for others' journeys—qualities directly developed through his painful failure.
- **Teaching and mentoring:** The capacity to help others navigate similar territories without requiring them to make identical mistakes. Michael now facilitates a family support group where he shares his hard-earned wisdom, helping others avoid the specific pitfalls he encountered.

What distinguishes leaders who transform failure into wisdom from those who simply accumulate painful experiences? Research on resilience and post-traumatic growth suggests several key mindsets:

- **Ownership without self-blame:** Taking responsibility for one's role in failure without descending into harsh self-judgment. Effective leaders distinguish between "I made a mistake" and "I am a mistake."
- **Curiosity over certainty:** Approaching failure with genuine wondering rather than premature conclusions. Questions like "What was I missing?" and, "What assumptions led me astray?" generate deeper insights than defensive certainty.
- **Future focus:** Orienting primarily toward how the failure experience can improve future actions rather than ruminating endlessly on past events. While reflection is necessary, its purpose is forward movement.
- **Community engagement:** Willingly sharing failure stories rather than hiding them, allowing collective wisdom to develop through shared experience. The vulnerability involved in acknowledging failure often creates deeper connection than displays of perfect competence.

I experienced this transformation myself when my initial attempts to rebuild my career in America met with repeated rejection. Each "no" felt like a personal judgment, confirming my fears that I had sacrificed my professional identity permanently by leaving Venezuela. The wisdom emerged slowly, through conversations with other immigrants who had successfully rebuilt careers and through my own painful reflection.

I eventually recognized that my approach was fundamentally flawed—I was trying to replicate my old professional identity rather than building something new that integrated my past experience with present reality. This hard-earned wisdom not only transformed my own career journey but has become central to how I mentor newer immigrants. The failures that once seemed like evidence of my inadequacy have become the foundation of insight that now benefits others.

Guiding Others Through the Storm: Leadership in Crisis

When crisis strikes, leadership takes on its most demanding and consequential form. Whether facing a family medical emergency, neighborhood disaster, or community tragedy, those who step forward to guide others through collective challenges demonstrate a distinct form of resilience. This leadership happens not despite the leader's pain but partly through it—the leader's authentic engagement with difficult realities creates a pathway for others to process their own experience.

Javier's response following a devastating hurricane in our community provides a powerful example. Having lost his own home to the storm, he was experiencing the same devastation as his neighbors. Yet rather than retreating into private grief, he emerged as an unexpected community coordinator—organizing shelter, connecting resources, and perhaps most importantly, creating space for collective emotional processing.

"I'm hurting just like all of you," he acknowledged at an impromptu gathering in a church basement that had become temporary housing. "But we've survived other storms, literal and figurative, and we'll get through this one together." His willingness to acknowledge his own pain while simultaneously conveying realistic hope created a container for others' complex emotions.

In the days that followed, Javier demonstrated several key principles of crisis leadership:

Presence: He was physically present in the most affected areas, listening to stories, embracing neighbors, and witnessing the full scope of the damage. This willingness to be proximate to suffering rather than remote from it built trust and demonstrated genuine care.

Decisive action: He organized clean-up teams, coordinated with official relief agencies, and established communication networks that kept everyone informed. This action-oriented approach channeled collective grief toward constructive activity.

Emotional authenticity: He allowed his genuine empathy to show without becoming overwhelmed by it. At community meetings, he acknowledged his own struggles while maintaining focus on the collective needs. This authentic balance made his strength more credible.

Meaning-making: Perhaps most importantly, he helped community members make meaning of the disaster, framing it not as random devastation but as an opportunity to demonstrate their values of mutual care and resilience. By connecting the crisis to their shared identity as a community that takes care of its own, he transformed a potentially atomizing experience into one that actually strengthened social bonds.

These elements—presence, action, authenticity, and meaning making—form the core of effective crisis leadership. They transform collective pain from a potentially destructive force into a catalyst for cohesion and renewal.

Research on public leadership during collective trauma confirms these observations. During crisis, people look to leaders not primarily for technical solutions but for three fundamental needs:

- **Direction:** Amid chaos, people need orientation—a clear sense of priorities and next steps that reduces overwhelming complexity to manageable action.
- **Connection:** Crisis threatens social bonds, but effective leaders reaffirm connection through both symbolic gestures and tangible solidarity.
- **Meaning:** Perhaps most fundamentally, people need help making sense of suffering—a framework that places pain within a larger narrative of purpose and values.

When leaders provide these elements, they help transform collective trauma from something merely endured into something potentially transformative. Rather than being diminished by crisis, communities can emerge with a stronger identity and clearer purpose.

This transformative leadership requires navigating the tension between acknowledging reality and instilling hope—what leadership scholar Ronald Heifetz calls "regulating the distress." Leaders who minimize pain lose credibility; those who only amplify it without perspective induce paralysis. The balanced approach acknowledges the full reality while maintaining focus on response capacity and future possibility.

In my own community work with refugee families, I've found that this balance is achieved not through pretending things aren't difficult, but through connecting current challenges to stories of previous resilience. "Remember how we navigated the asylum process," I might say. "This housing crisis is another mountain to climb, but we've climbed mountains before." This narrative continuity neither minimizes the present difficulty nor allows it to appear insurmountable.

The leadership that emerges through crisis can permanently alter someone's role in a family or community. Individuals who never saw themselves as leaders often discover capacities that continue to benefit others long after the immediate emergency passes. The grandmother who organizes family response during a medical crisis may become the ongoing emotional anchor for younger generations. The neighbor who coordinates block-level disaster response may evolve into the person who organizes community improvement projects in normal times.

Perhaps most powerfully, crisis leadership often creates cascading resilience—those who were guided through difficulty by an effective leader frequently develop leadership capacities themselves, creating ripples of influence that extend far beyond the original event.

The Emotional Labor of Leadership: Sustaining Yourself While Supporting Others

Leadership that emerges from personal pain carries unique rewards but also distinct challenges. Supporting others through difficulty while still processing your own suffering requires particular attention to sustainable practices. Without this attention, even the most well-intentioned leaders risk burning out, potentially causing harm to themselves and those they seek to help.

When Rosalind's daughter was diagnosed with autism, her own grief and adjustment process was still fresh when other parents began seeking her guidance. "I became a resource for newly diagnosed families before I had fully processed my own emotions," she told me. "While supporting others gave my experience meaning, I wasn't prepared for how it would continually reactivate my own pain."

This phenomenon—what psychologists call *compassion fatigue* or *secondary trauma*—represents a significant risk for leaders whose work touches areas of their own wounding. The emotional labor of supporting others through terrain that remains tender in one's own experience requires deliberate practices of self-care and boundary setting.

Several approaches help maintain sustainable leadership that emerges from personal pain:

Integration before guidance: While our suffering doesn't need to be completely resolved before we can support others (indeed, ongoing struggle often provides authenticity), some degree of integration should precede guidance. As trauma expert Judith Herman notes, "The survivor who has achieved some stable ground is in a position to offer help to others; the survivor who is still struggling with the basic tasks of safety usually is not."

For Rosalind, this meant working with a therapist and participating in a support group as a member before stepping into a leadership role. These spaces allowed her to process her raw emotions and begin constructing meaning from her experience before taking responsibility for others' journeys.

Bounded engagement: Effective leaders recognize that sustainable support requires clear parameters. This might mean limited hours, specific contexts, or particular roles that allow them to contribute without becoming depleted.

Jason, whose son died by suicide, eventually became a grief support group facilitator—but only after establishing clear boundaries. "I limit my facilitation to twice monthly, and I have specific self-care rituals before and after each session," he explained. "Without those boundaries, I couldn't sustain this work."

Ongoing support: Leaders who emerge through pain benefit tremendously from maintaining their own support networks even as they support others. This creates channels for processing the emotional weight of leadership rather than carrying it alone.

Elena, the immigrant community leader mentioned earlier, participates in a monthly "leaders' circle" where those supporting others can share their own challenges in a confidential space. "Having somewhere I can be vulnerable about how hard this work sometimes feels makes it possible for me to continue," she reflected.

Growth through service: While leadership that emerges from pain involves genuine giving to others, it can simultaneously support the leader's ongoing healing process. Many leaders report that supporting others continues to deepen their own integration and meaning making.

When Teresa began mentoring mothers who had experienced pregnancy loss similar to her own, she discovered that each conversation added layers to her understanding. "Hearing others' stories helps me continue making sense of my own," she noted. "It's not just me giving to them—there's a reciprocity that nourishes me."

This reciprocity points to a broader truth: the boundary between helping others and helping oneself is often more permeable than we might assume. In healthy leadership contexts, the act of guiding others simultaneously strengthens the guide. As Holocaust survivor and psychiatrist Viktor Frankl observed, "Self-actualization is possible only as a side-effect of self-transcendence"—meaning that we often find our greatest personal healing through service to something beyond ourselves.

I experienced this paradox deeply in my work with newly arrived Venezuelan immigrants. Even as I offered practical guidance on navigating American systems, each conversation was also healing something in me—reconnecting me to my cultural identity, allowing me to transform painful experiences into useful wisdom, and creating meaning from circumstances that had once seemed merely destructive. My leadership role became not just a way of helping others but a central avenue for my own continued integration and growth.

This phenomenon—where leadership born of suffering becomes a vehicle for mutual transformation—represents one of the most hopeful dimensions of the pain-to-power journey. The very act of extending ourselves to others in their pain can become a powerful catalyst for our own healing, creating virtuous cycles of growth and service.

Everyday Leadership: Small Acts with Ripple Effects

Leadership that emerges from personal pain isn't limited to formal roles or dramatic circumstances. Often it manifests in small daily actions that influence those around us—a timely word of encouragement informed by our own struggles, a different approach to parenting based on what we wished we'd received, or simple modeling of resilient responses to everyday setbacks.

These micro-leadership moments may seem insignificant in isolation, but their cumulative impact can profoundly shape families, friendships, workplaces, and communities. Like small rudder adjustments that eventually change a ship's destination, these everyday leadership choices—informed by our transformed relationship with pain—can redirect cultural patterns and shift collective possibilities.

Consider these everyday leadership opportunities that emerge from our personal pain-to-power journey:

Transparent coping: Simply demonstrating healthy responses to difficulties—neither hiding our struggles nor being defined by them—provides powerful modeling for others, particularly children and young people. When parents navigate disappointment with authentic emotion followed by constructive action, they teach resilience more effectively than any lecture could.

Damien, who grew up with a father who concealed all vulnerability, made a conscious choice to show his children appropriate emotional honesty. "When I lost a job I'd worked hard for, I let them see both my disappointment and my problem-solving," he explained. "I wanted them to know that setbacks hurt but don't have to destroy you."

Language offering: Those who have transformed their relationship with pain often develop nuanced language for experiences that others struggle to articulate. Offering this language—naming feelings, processes, or possibilities that might otherwise remain nebulous—can be profoundly relieving to those still searching for words.

When Cynthia described her grief process to a newly widowed friend, she shared language that had helped her: "It's not that time heals all wounds; it's that you gradually build a life around the wound." Her friend later told her that this framing had been transformative, giving her permission to stop waiting for the pain to disappear while still moving forward.

Boundary modeling: Many who have transformed suffering into strength have learned crucial lessons about boundaries—when to say no, how to protect energy, what constitutes healthy support versus unhealthy caretaking. Demonstrating these boundaries offers others permission and patterns for their own limit-setting.

Marco, who burned out trying to solve his sister's addiction problems, now shares his hard-earned wisdom with friends facing similar situations: "You can love someone without trying to manage their recovery." This simple distinction has helped numerous others avoid the exhausting trap of over-responsibility.

Redemptive storytelling: How we narrate our painful experiences profoundly influences those around us. Sharing stories that acknowledge real suffering while also highlighting growth, meaning, and possibility creates templates that others can adapt to their own circumstances.

Leila's approach to discussing her cancer journey evolved from "Why me?" to "What now?" narratives. Her willingness to share this evolution has influenced how her extended family discusses challenges, gradually shifting their collective storytelling from victimhood toward agency.

These everyday leadership moments don't require special positions or dramatic interventions. They simply involve allowing our transformed relationship with pain to naturally influence our interactions, creating ripples that extend far beyond our immediate experience.

I practice this kind of everyday leadership when mentoring young immigrants. Rather than positioning myself as someone who has "arrived" at some perfect resolution, I share ongoing challenges alongside growth, normalizing the non-linear nature of adaptation. "I still have days when I miss home so much it hurts to breathe," I might tell someone struggling with homesickness. "And I've also built a meaningful life here that I wouldn't trade. Both are true." This honest complexity creates space for others to hold their own contradictions without shame.

These micro-leadership opportunities emerge naturally from the inner work we've discussed throughout previous chapters. As we develop mindfulness, meaning-making capacity, cognitive flexibility, and emotional integration, our external interactions organically shift. We need not strive to influence others; we simply allow our transformed relationship with pain to manifest in how we move through the world.

This everyday leadership powerfully illustrates how personal transformation inevitably becomes social transformation. Each individual who converts their suffering into wisdom creates possibilities for others to do the same. These overlapping ripples of influence gradually shift cultural patterns around pain, resilience, and growth.

Pain-to-Power Exercises – Chapter 10

1. Leadership crucible mapping: Reflect on a significant challenge you've faced that has provided you with wisdom you can now offer others. On paper, create a diagram with three columns: "What was painful," "What I learned," and "How I can help others." In the first column, honestly acknowledge the difficulties. In the second, identify specific insights that emerged from those difficulties. In the third, describe how you might share these insights to support others facing similar challenges. This exercise helps you recognize how your pain has already developed potential leadership wisdom and how it might serve beyond your personal growth. By documenting this pattern, you develop confidence that your difficulties aren't just obstacles but formative experiences that equip you to guide others.

2. Wisdom offering identification: Consider a specific community, relationship, or context where your "pain-transformed-to-wisdom might be helpful to others. This could be family relationships, a friend group, a support community, or a formal organization. List three specific insights from your journey that might benefit others in this context. Then, for each insight, identify a concrete, appropriate way you might share it—perhaps through a conversation, a written reflection, a group discussion, or simply modeling a different approach. Remember that effective wisdom-sharing usually happens through invitation rather than imposition. This exercise helps you translate personal growth into helpful guidance for others while respecting their autonomy.

3. Sustainable Leadership Check: If you're already in a position where you support others through difficulties similar to your own past or present pain, assess your current sustainability. Create a grid with four categories: "Energy Drains," "Energy Sources," "Current Boundaries," and "Needed Boundaries." Under each, list relevant factors in your leadership role. This assessment helps create sustainable patterns that allow you to continue supporting others without depleting yourself. Remember that your leadership will be most effective and long-lasting when it emerges from a place of genuine strength rather than obligation or depletion. Adjust your approach based on this assessment, perhaps implementing new boundaries or support structures that allow your leadership to flourish without burnout.

Having explored how our transformed relationship with pain can develop leadership capacity, let's now examine how technology can either hinder or help our pain-to-power journey. The next chapter explores practical digital tools and approaches for building resilience, finding meaning, and connecting authentically—even in our hyperconnected world where technology itself can become both a source of suffering and a potential ally for growth.

CHAPTER 11

Digital Tools for Transformation

*Technology as an Ally in Your
Pain-to-Power Journey*

Harnessing Technology to Support Your Resilience and Growth

In a bustling café, I sat surrounded by screen-lit faces—each physically present yet mentally elsewhere. I caught myself compulsively checking my phone for Venezuela political updates while attempting to draft an important email, my attention fragmented between worlds. Having fled the very real dangers of my homeland, I found myself pondering a strange irony: How had this virtual world become its own source of both suffering and potential healing? And more importantly, how could I—how could we all—harness digital tools to support rather than undermine our journey from pain to power?

Throughout this book, we've explored numerous practices for transforming suffering into strength—from mindfulness and cognitive reframing to physical engagement and meaning making. Yet the reality of modern life is that much of our experience now unfolds through digital technologies. Rather than viewing this digital dimension as separate from our resilience journey, this chapter explores how we can intentionally use technology as an ally in our transformation.

The Digital Paradox in Healing

Before exploring specific digital resources, we must acknowledge an important tension: the same technologies that can support our healing often contribute to our suffering. Social media platforms that connect us to supportive communities can also trigger comparison and anxiety. Devices that provide access to resilience tools can simultaneously fragment our attention and disrupt our sleep. This paradox requires us to approach digital resources with both intention and discernment.

During my own adaptation to America, I noticed how video calls with family in Venezuela both sustained me emotionally and sometimes deepened my homesickness. News apps kept me informed about my country's situation yet often left me feeling helpless and anxious. These contradictory effects weren't random—they reflected specific patterns in how I engaged with these technologies.

The difference between technology that heals and technology that harms lies not primarily in which tools we use, but in how we use them. Three key elements transform digital engagement from potentially harmful to genuinely supportive:

- **Intentional purpose:** Approaching technology with a clear purpose rather than a habitual reaction directs our engagement toward specific resilience goals rather than mindless consumption.
- **Attentional boundaries:** Establishing when, where, and how we engage with digital tools preserves our capacity for presence and prevents technology from colonizing our entire attention landscape.
- **Integrated practice:** Using digital tools to enhance rather than replace direct experience creates a harmonious relationship between our virtual and physical worlds.

With these principles in mind, let's explore how digital resources can support your resilience at different stages of your pain-to-power journey.

Tools for Crisis Moments: Digital Support When You're Overwhelmed

When we're in acute distress—whether from grief, anxiety, trauma triggers, or other overwhelming experiences—our cognitive capacity often narrows dramatically. During these moments, simple, accessible digital tools can provide immediate stabilization support.

After learning of particularly disturbing news from Venezuela, I sometimes experienced panic attacks that made it difficult to think clearly or function effectively. A simple breathing guidance app became my digital anchor during these episodes—requiring minimal cognitive effort yet effectively guiding my physiological response back toward regulation.

Several digital approaches can provide similar support during your most difficult moments:

Grounding and regulation apps: Applications like Breathe, Calm Harm, and What's Up offer immediate exercises for managing overwhelming emotions. These tools provide structured guidance when your own internal resources feel depleted.

For maximum effectiveness during crisis moments:

- Familiarize yourself with these tools during calmer periods so they're easily accessible when needed.
- Consider placing shortcuts to specific exercises on your phone's home screen for one-touch access.
- Use tools that require minimal reading or complex interaction during acute distress.

Crisis text lines and support chats: Services like Crisis Text Line (text HOME to 741741) and 7 Cups provide immediate connection with trained responders or listeners when isolation compounds suffering.

When I felt particularly alone in my early immigration experience, a text-based support service allowed me to express my distress and receive a human response without needing to manage a full voice conversation—something that would have been too challenging during those moments of intense emotion.

Sensory-soothing resources: Apps providing calming sounds, visuals, or interactive experiences can help regulate your nervous system when you're overwhelmed. Tools like Relax Melodies, Silk interactive art, or even simple nature videos can engage your senses in ways that gently shift your physiological state.

When not to use digital tools during crisis: It's crucial to recognize when technology might hinder rather than help. During the most acute trauma responses or profound grief, screens may create an unhelpful distance from necessary emotional processing. In these moments, if possible, direct human contact or physical grounding activities (feeling the floor beneath your feet, wrapping yourself in a blanket, placing your hand on your heart) often provide more effective support than digital mediation.

Tools for Daily Practice: Building Resilience Through Consistent Engagement

Beyond crisis moments, the foundation of resilience develops through consistent practice. Digital tools can significantly enhance this daily work by providing structure, accountability, and integrated support for the core practices we've explored throughout this book.

When establishing my new life in America, I found that the most powerful digital supports weren't those I used occasionally during acute distress, but those that helped me maintain consistent resilience practices despite the chaos of adaptation. A simple meditation timer with progress tracking transformed my sporadic practice into a daily anchor that gradually expanded my distress tolerance and present-moment awareness.

Consider these digital approaches for supporting your daily resilience development:

Mindfulness and meditation support: Apps like Insight Timer, Healthy Minds, and Waking Up provide structured guidance for developing present-moment awareness—a fundamental skill for transforming your relationship with pain.

Rather than recommending specific apps (which change frequently), look for these key features:

- Variety of practice lengths (including very brief options for challenging days)
- Guidance specifically addressing difficult emotions and experiences
- Progress tracking that motivates consistency without creating unhelpful pressure
- Options for both guided and unguided practice as your skills develop

Journaling platforms: Digital journaling tools like Day One, Journey, or simple note applications provide accessible ways to implement the reflection practices discussed in cChapter 6.

During my adaptation to America, I developed a hybrid approach—using digital journaling for brief daily entries that captured immediate experiences, complemented by deeper handwritten reflection weekly. This combination provided both accessibility for consistent documentation and the embodied processing that comes through physical writing.

Habit Development Systems: Apps like Habitica, Streaks, or Done help establish and maintain the consistent practices that build resilience over time.

When implementing these tools:

- Start with just one or two resilience habits rather than attempting a complete system immediately.
- Link new digital habits to existing daily anchors (like checking a gratitude prompt with morning coffee).
- Use visual tracking to maintain motivation through the challenging early phases of habit formation.

Community connection platforms: Tools like Circles, Mighty Networks, or even simple group chats provide ongoing connection with others with similar experiences—a crucial component of sustainable resilience.

When to choose non-digital alternatives: While these tools can powerfully support daily practice, be attentive to when screen fatigue or digital overwhelm suggests a need for low-tech alternatives. If you spend your workday on screens, consider physical journaling, in-person groups, or audio-only guidance for your resilience practices to provide cognitive-attentional contrast.

Tools for Reflection and Integration: Making Meaning of Your Journey

Some of our most significant resilience development occurs not in crisis moments or daily practice, but through periodic reflection that helps us integrate our experiences and extract meaning from our challenges. Digital tools can create structured space for this deeper work, especially when integrated with the meaning-making approaches discussed in chapter 4.

After several years in America, I realized I had been so focused on survival and adaptation that I had rarely stepped back to reflect on the larger meaning of my journey. A digital life review platform prompted me to examine patterns across seemingly disconnected experiences, helping me recognize how my exile had developed capacities I might never have discovered otherwise. This structured reflection transformed how I understood my own story—not just as loss and displacement, but as a unique path toward purpose and contribution.

Consider these digital approaches for supporting deeper reflection and meaning making:

Structured reflection guides: Applications like Reflection.app, Day One's guided prompts, or ReflectLy provide frameworks for examining your experiences through resilience-oriented lenses.

Effective reflection platforms typically include the following:

- Questions that prompt a connection between current challenges and larger values
- Frameworks for recognizing patterns across different experiences
- Opportunities to articulate emerging meaning and purpose
- Ways to track your evolving narrative over time

Timeline and life mapping tools: Applications like Timeline, Daylio (with its pattern recognition features), or even digital photo collections with journaling capabilities help visualize your journey and identify important transitions and transformative moments.

When my memories of Venezuela began fading—a common but painful experience for immigrants—a digital timeline project helped me integrate my past and present in a coherent narrative that honored both where I came from and who I was becoming. This integration significantly enhanced my sense of continuity and meaning amid radical transition.

Values clarification resources: Tools like Values Clarity, Checkpoint, or specialized coaches' platforms offer interactive exercises for identifying core values and assessing alignment between daily choices and deeper principles—a crucial process for finding meaning amid difficulty.

Legacy and wisdom-capture systems: Platforms like StoryCorps, Memories, or various digital storytelling applications help transform difficult experiences into meaningful narratives that can be shared with others or preserved for personal reflection.

Implementation Guidance for Reflection Tools:

- Schedule specific times for deeper reflection rather than attempting it in fragmented moments.
- Create environmental conditions that support presence (silence notifications, use comfortable seating, perhaps light a candle) even when using digital tools.

- Consider periodic technology fasts before significant reflection sessions to create mental space.
- Balance digital reflection with embodied integration through movement, nature exposure, or artistic expression.

When Technology Helps vs. When It Hinders: Practical Guidelines

Throughout this exploration of digital tools, an important question emerges: How do we determine when technology is supporting our resilience versus undermining it? Rather than providing absolute rules, consider these contextual guidelines based on both research and lived experience:

Technology Tends to Help When It Does the Following:

- Provides structure for practices you value but struggle to maintain independently
- Connects you with others who share your specific challenges when local support is limited
- Offers expertise or guidance unavailable in your immediate environment
- Creates helpful distance from overwhelming emotions during acute distress
- Makes tracking patterns and progress possible in ways memory alone cannot
- Enhances rather than replaces direct experience and human connection

Technology Tends to Hinder When It Does the Following:

- Becomes a primary means of avoiding uncomfortable emotions rather than processing them
- Consistently leaves you feeling worse (more anxious, inadequate, or depleted) after engagement
- Fragments your attention to the point that you struggle to be fully present in important moments

- Creates isolation from physical community and direct human contact
- Generates additional stress through complexity, technical problems, or constant interruptions
- Becomes something you feel dependent upon rather than empowered by

I discovered these distinctions through difficult experiences during my adaptation to America. Video calls with family initially provided crucial emotional sustenance, but when they became a way to mentally "live in Venezuela" rather than build my new life, they actually hindered my integration. News consumption that helped me stay informed and connected became problematic when it evolved into compulsive checking that increased my sense of helplessness without improving my ability to contribute meaningfully.

The key is developing discernment—the capacity to notice how specific technological engagements affect your resilience and adjust accordingly. This discernment develops through regular reflection on questions like:

- How do I feel after using this digital tool? More resourced or more depleted?
- Is this technology enhancing my direct experience or replacing it?
- Does this digital engagement serve my deeper values and priorities or distract from them?
- Am I using this tool with intention or reacting to its design features and notifications?

This discernment isn't about achieving perfect technological hygiene, but about continuously refining your relationship with digital tools to better serve your resilience and well-being.

Creating Your Personal Digital Resilience Ecosystem

Rather than approaching digital tools as isolated resources, consider developing an integrated ecosystem of technologies that work together to support different aspects of your resilience journey. This ecosystem will be highly personal, reflecting your specific needs, preferences, and circumstances.

When I finally developed a coherent digital support system for my adaptation journey, it included these interconnected elements:

- A meditation app for daily practice and acute stress management
- A simple journaling platform synchronized across devices
- A secure group chat with fellow Venezuelan immigrants for mutual support
- A news curation service that provided important updates without overwhelming me
- Regular video connections with family during scheduled times that supported rather than hindered my integration
- Digital boundary tools that protected my attention from fragmentation

This ecosystem evolved through experimentation rather than emerging fully formed. I discovered what worked by noticing what actually supported my resilience rather than what promised to do so.

To develop your own digital resilience ecosystem:

Start with your specific challenges: Rather than adopting tools because they're popular or highly rated, identify your particular resilience challenges and seek technologies specifically addressing those needs.

For example, if social isolation compounds your depression, prioritize meaningful connection platforms. If rumination disrupts your sleep, focus on evening mindfulness and boundary-setting tools. If emotional regulation is your primary struggle, emphasize applications supporting that specific capacity.

Consider your access points and triggers: Identify when and where you most need support, ensuring your digital tools are accessible in those moments and contexts.

Before boarding flights—a time when I often experienced travel anxiety—I learned to download specific guided meditations for takeoff, midflight, and landing. This preparation ensured support was available precisely when connectivity would be unavailable and stress most likely.

Build in boundaries from the beginning: As you adopt new digital tools, simultaneously establish parameters around their use to prevent the technology itself from becoming a source of stress or dependency.

For each new application I adopted, I determined specific usage contexts (when, where, and how I would engage with it) and regular evaluation points to assess whether it was truly serving my resilience or potentially undermining it.

Create intentional integration points: Look for ways your digital tools can complement and enhance your non-digital resilience practices rather than replacing them.

My digital journaling platform included a feature that compiled entries into a printable format, allowing me to periodically review and reflect on physical copies that engaged different cognitive and emotional processes than screen reading.

Cultural and contextual considerations: While smartphone access has expanded globally, digital resilience tools remain unevenly distributed across cultural and socioeconomic contexts. Community-based adaptations—like shared devices or simplified applications—can extend these benefits in diverse environments.

In my work with recently arrived immigrants with limited technological access, we've developed approaches like community device libraries, simplified applications with minimal language requirements, and hybrid systems combining digital and traditional resources to ensure resilience support remains accessible regardless of technological circumstances.

The Role of Human Connection in Digital Resilience

Throughout this exploration of digital tools, one principle remains paramount: technology serves resilience most effectively when it enhances rather than replaces human connection. The most sophisticated application cannot substitute for being truly seen and heard by another person who understands your struggle.

My most powerful resilience support came not from any particular technology but from how digital tools facilitated deeper human connections. Video calls didn't replace in-person relationships, but sustained them across geographical separation. Online forums didn't substitute for direct conversation, but connected me with others who shared my specific experiences when local understanding was limited.

As you develop your digital resilience toolkit, consider these principles for maintaining the primacy of human connection:

Use technology as a bridge, not a destination: Approach digital tools as means of facilitating connection rather than as ends in themselves. Online support groups are most effective when they eventually encourage direct relationships; digital communication works best when it supplements rather than replaces in-person interaction.

Prioritize interactive over passive engagement: Technologies that involve active participation and exchange generally support resilience more effectively than those encouraging passive consumption. Contributing to a discussion forum typically provides a greater benefit than simply reading posts; interactive meditation guidance usually creates more engagement than watching meditation videos.

Balance convenience with presence: While digital tools offer tremendous convenience, sometimes the additional effort of direct connection creates valuable friction that enhances presence and commitment. Consider occasionally choosing a phone call over a text exchange or an in-person meeting over video chat, especially for emotionally significant conversations.

Create digital-free connection spaces: Designate regular times and contexts where connection occurs without technological mediation—meals without devices, walks without phones, gatherings where technology remains peripheral rather than central. These digital-free zones preserve our capacity for the full-bandwidth human interaction that forms the foundation of resilience.

Final Thoughts: Technology as Servant, Not Master

The digital transformation of our world offers unprecedented opportunities for supporting resilience while simultaneously presenting unique challenges to our well-being. The key to navigating this landscape lies not in the categorical embrace or rejection of technology, but in developing a discerning, intentional relationship with digital tools—one where technology serves our humanity rather than diminishing it.

My journey from Venezuela to America coincided with extraordinary technological transformation—from calling cards and occasional emails to smartphones and constant connectivity. This parallel evolution taught me that neither nostalgic technophobia nor uncritical techno-optimism serves true resilience. Instead, we need a balanced approach that harnesses technology's potential while remaining grounded in the fundamentally human capacities that constitute our deepest strength.

As you continue your pain-to-power journey, I encourage you to approach digital tools with both openness and discernment—exploring their possibilities while maintaining clear boundaries, leveraging their strengths while honoring their limitations, and always keeping them in service to your deeper values and connections.

The most powerful technology for transformation remains your own human capacity for presence, meaning making, and connection. Digital tools, at their best, simply support and amplify these fundamentally human processes— providing structure, accessibility, and enhancement without replacement or diminishment.

In this spirit of balanced integration, the digital dimension becomes not a distracting tangent from your resilience journey but a valuable supporting thread—one element in the rich tapestry of resources that can help transform your pain into authentic, lasting power.

Pain-to-Power Exercises – Chapter 11

1. Digital resilience audit: Examine your current technology use through the lens of resilience development. Create a chart with three columns: "Digital Tools I Currently Use," "How They Support My Resilience," and "How They Might Undermine My Resilience." List your most-used applications, platforms, and digital habits in the first column. For each entry, complete the second and third columns with an honest assessment. This exercise helps you recognize which digital elements genuinely serve your pain-to-power journey versus those that may be hindering it. Based on this audit, identify three specific changes to implement—perhaps adopting a new supportive tool, modifying how you use an existing platform, or establishing boundaries around a potentially depleting habit.

2. Crisis moment preparation: Identify three specific situations when you're most likely to feel overwhelmed (perhaps grief triggers, anxiety spikes, or particular stressors). For each situation, select one digital tool that could provide immediate support, and prepare it for crisis-moment access: download the application, create necessary accounts, explore its features during a calm period, and place it in an easily accessible location on your device. Then create a simple if-then plan: "If I experience [specific overwhelming situation], then I will use [specific digital tool] for support." This preparation ensures you have appropriate resources readily available when cognitive capacity is most limited, transforming potential crisis moments into opportunities for practicing regulation rather than spiraling into overwhelm.

3. Boundary implementation experiment: Select one area where technology may be undermining rather than supporting your resilience (perhaps sleep disruption from late-night scrolling, comparison triggers from social media, or attention fragmentation from constant notifications). Design a two-week experiment implementing a specific boundary in this area—perhaps a technology curfew, selective notification settings, or designated engagement periods. Document both the challenges you encounter and the benefits you notice, particularly how this boundary affects your resilience practices and overall well-being. This experimental approach helps you discover personalized boundaries that enhance your relationship with technology without requiring dramatic digital detox or generating resistance that undermines sustainable change.

As we've explored how technology can support your pain-to-power journey when approached with intention and discernment, we come to our final chapter—an exploration of how resilience development unfolds throughout your lifetime, continuing to deepen its impact both within you and through your influence on others. We'll examine how resilience becomes not just a response to difficulty but a fundamental orientation to life itself, creating ripples of transformation that extend far beyond your individual experience.

CHAPTER 12

Embracing the Future

Pain as a Portal – Lifelong Growth and Building a Resilient World

One stormy Alabama night, thunder and rain stirred me—not with dread, but with unexpected memory. The humid air and booming echoes transported me back to my childhood in Caracas. For a moment, I existed in both worlds—my American present and Venezuelan past—connected by sensory experience. This moment revealed something profound about integration: the pain of exile hadn't simply disappeared; it had transformed into a bridge connecting different parts of my identity. The storm-chasing child, the freedom fighter who left everything behind, and the exile building a new life—all these versions of myself coexisted in that sensory memory, united by the journey between them.

As we arrive at this final chapter, we turn our eyes forward. How do we continue to embrace pain as a tool for continuous growth throughout our lives? How do we share what we've learned with others, particularly the next generation? How might communities and societies use the crucible of collective pain to transform and advance?

This chapter is about hope and proactive resilience. It's about understanding that the journey of turning pain into power doesn't end with recovery from any single difficult experience. Life will always present new challenges, so resilience is not a one-time achievement but a lifelong practice. However, each time we overcome, we become better equipped for the next wave. Embracing the future means leaning into that truth: that change (often born through discomfort) is constant, and if we stay open to learning, we can greet each change not with dread but with a spirit of adaptation and even optimism.

Lifelong Resilience: The Evolving You

Think back to who you were ten years ago. What challenges seemed insurmountable then that you now take in stride? What coping strategies have you developed that your younger self couldn't imagine? How has your understanding of pain and difficulty evolved? If you're like most people, the comparison reveals not just change but growth—an expansion of capacity that came precisely through confronting difficulties.

This evolution doesn't stop. The you of the future will have weathered storms you might not see coming and will have discovered new capacities the current you can't yet imagine. This continuous development represents the heart of lifelong resilience—not a fixed trait but an ever-evolving set of capabilities and perspectives that grows with each challenge successfully navigated.

Recent research in post-traumatic growth highlights how this process works. After significant adversity, many people report positive changes in five key areas:

- **Personal strength:** A greater sense of capability and self-reliance
- **New possibilities:** Recognition of new paths and opportunities
- **Relationships**: Deeper connections and greater appreciation for others
- **Life appreciation:** Enhanced gratitude for life itself
- **Spiritual/existential growth:** Deeper understanding of meaning and purpose

These growth areas don't emerge immediately but develop through ongoing reflection and integration of difficult experiences. The painful event itself doesn't create growth; rather, our continued engagement with its meaning does.

Importantly, resilience is not linear. There may be times when you feel very strong and times when you feel knocked down again. This fluctuation is normal

170

and natural. One setback doesn't mean you've lost your resilience; it means you're human and need to regroup. Because you have overcome before, you can have confidence you will overcome again.

I experienced this non-linearity powerfully when I lost a close family member several years after establishing myself in America. The grief temporarily collapsed many of my hard-won coping strategies. For a time, I feared I had somehow lost my resilience. What I eventually realized was that I wasn't starting from scratch—I was applying my resilience to a new form of pain. Gradually, I found my way forward, integrating this loss into my life story just as I had integrated other difficulties.

Adaptability emerges as perhaps the key trait of lifelong resilience. Embracing the future means expecting the unexpected and being willing to adjust your sails. It doesn't mean you don't feel sad or scared about changes or losses, but it means you don't cling too tightly to the past or how things "should be." Instead, you acknowledge reality and then ask, "Given this new reality, how can I make the best of it?" That question is empowering because it moves you from resistance to a creative response.

Research on successful aging particularly emphasizes this adaptability. Dr. George Vaillant's landmark Harvard Study of Adult Development found that those who maintained well-being into advanced age weren't those who avoided difficulty but those who continued adapting to life's changing circumstances. They adjusted goals when necessary, found new sources of meaning when old ones became unavailable, and maintained capacity for joy even amid loss.

Passing the Torch: Helping Others and the Next Generation

When I first began volunteering with recently arrived Venezuelan immigrants, I approached the role with some trepidation. Would sharing my own difficult immigration experience help or overwhelm them? What I discovered surprised me: the simple act of me saying, "I've been where you are, and while it's genuinely hard, there is a path forward," created visible relief for them. Not because it magically solved their problems, but because it transformed their narrative from, "I'm alone in impossible circumstances," to, "Others have walked this path before me."

This experience taught me something powerful about resilience: it multiplies when shared. As you grow stronger through your own challenges, you become a beacon for others facing similar difficulties. Your transformed pain becomes not just personal strength but a light illuminating possible paths for those still finding their way.

Psychologists call this phenomenon *resilience modeling*, and research demonstrates its remarkable impact across contexts. Children who witness adults calmly navigate setbacks develop greater stress tolerance than those whose adults catastrophize challenges. Patients newly diagnosed with serious illness show better coping when connected with others who have successfully managed the same condition. Our brains contain specialized *mirror neurons* that activate when we observe others' actions and emotions, creating internal representations that facilitate learning.

We can intentionally share resilience wisdom through several powerful approaches:

- **Authentic storytelling:** Sharing your own journey through difficulty—including both the struggles and the strategies that helped—provides others with both hope and practical guidance.
- **Contextual mentoring:** Formal or informal mentoring relationships create space for tailored resilience transmission. Effective resilience mentors don't position themselves as having "arrived" at some perfect resilience state but rather as fellow travelers who have navigated similar terrain.
- **Environmental design:** Perhaps most powerfully, we can create environments that nurture resilience in others—whether in families, workplaces, schools, or communities. This involves developing contexts that balance challenge with support, normalize struggle as part of growth, and celebrate progress rather than just achievement.

The transmission of resilience to younger generations deserves particular attention. Children and young adults today face unique challenges—from climate anxiety to polarized social contexts to complex digital landscapes—that previous generations didn't encounter in the same forms. Effective intergenerational resilience transmission involves acknowledging these contexts while sharing timeless wisdom about navigating adversity.

My own approach to sharing resilience has evolved over time. Initially, I focused primarily on practical guidance—how to navigate immigration systems, find resources, and build networks. While this remains important, I've learned that the deeper transmission happens through the relationship itself—creating spaces where people feel truly seen in their struggle while simultaneously being reminded of their capacity. This balance of acknowledgment and empowerment constitutes the heart of resilience transmission.

The Never-Ending Story: Resilience as a Way of Life

During a particularly challenging period of adjustment after leaving my country, I found myself exhausted by the constant effort of adapting to a new culture, language, and identity. Would resilience always require such deliberate, draining effort? A wise mentor offered this perspective: "What feels like constant paddling upstream eventually becomes simply how you swim." His words proved prophetic. The coping strategies that once required conscious implementation gradually became natural responses; the meaning making that felt forced evolved into intuitive understanding. Resilience had transformed from something I did into something I was.

This integration represents the mature phase of resilience development—what researchers call *resilience as a way of life*. Rather than a collection of techniques applied during a crisis, resilience becomes an ongoing orientation to experience, a lens through which we perceive and respond to life's continual unfolding.

There is no final exam in resilience where you get a certificate and never have to worry again. But what changes over time is that you develop a sort of resilience muscle memory. The first major loss or failure you face might feel unbearable, but years later, after you've been through a few, you carry an implicit knowledge: "I survived that; I can survive this too." You might still feel intense emotions, but somewhere inside is a calm center that knows you will eventually be okay and even perhaps grow from this.

Research on long-term trauma survivors illustrates this integration process. Those who demonstrate sustained recovery and growth don't necessarily experience fewer difficulties than others; rather, they respond differently to them. Their responses show several distinctive qualities:

- **Flexible coping:** Rather than relying on a single approach to all challenges, they draw from a diverse repertoire of strategies calibrated to specific situations.
- **Values alignment:** Their choices during difficulty consistently reflect their core values rather than merely avoiding discomfort.
- **Balanced perspective:** They maintain awareness of both difficulty and possibility, pain and growth, limitations and resources.
- **Integrated narrative:** Perhaps most distinctively, they maintain an evolving life story that incorporates difficult experiences into a coherent, meaningful narrative.

Another aspect of resilience as a way of life is gratitude and savoring the good. When you've suffered, good times and good things shine even brighter. Many survivors say they learned to not sweat the small stuff and to value the present more. Embracing the future doesn't mean focusing only on challenges; it means also opening fully to joy when it comes. Pain teaches the value of its opposite: happiness, peace, and love.

Finally, consider seeing pain and growth as a cycle, much like the seasons. There will be winters in your life, cold and harsh. But spring does come, and with it blossoms—new parts of you born from what you endured. Embracing the future is recognizing this cycle and not fearing it as much. With each winter, you know spring is around the corner. With each spring, you know you are wiser from the winter that passed.

A Vision of Resilience

Picture yourself a few years or decades from now, having continued on this journey. What kind of person do you hope to be when facing pain then? Perhaps more patient, or more courageous, or more compassionate. The work you do now, and continue to do, step by step, is shaping that future self.

In my own vision, I see myself someday able to witness Venezuela's healing and transformation—whether I'm present physically or supporting from afar—with the hard-won wisdom my journey has provided. I imagine being able to offer both pragmatic guidance and emotional support to others navigating political upheaval, cultural transition, or identity reconstruction. This vision doesn't erase the pain of what happened but gives it purpose and context within a larger story of both personal and collective healing.

Also picture the ripple effect: by turning your pain into power, you will have influenced others—family, friends, and colleagues—to maybe handle their struggles a bit better, too, or at least to be inspired by your example. Pain can isolate, but overcoming it can unite. As more people adopt this resilient outlook, our communities and world become stronger together.

Imagine a world where instead of responding to crises with despair and division, we respond more and more with solidarity and innovation. It might sound idealistic, but it starts with individuals. It starts with how you respond to the next personal or shared crisis. Courage and hope are as contagious as fear and despair. Each person who transforms their own suffering into wisdom and strength becomes a node in an expanding network of resilience.

In embracing the future, let's conclude with a reminder: pain is not the enemy. It is a difficult teacher, but a teacher nonetheless. We don't go seeking it, but when it arrives, we don't need to run from it. We can face it, work with it, and allow it to transform us. When we do so, pain loses some of its sting because we know it can be turned to purpose.

Your story, with all its ups and downs, is important and meaningful. Every chapter, even the painful ones, adds to the richness of who you are. And who you are is someone capable of incredible strength, kindness, and growth.

As you step into the future, carry with you the knowledge that you are never alone in your suffering, that within every challenge lies an opportunity, and that your capacity for resilience is limitless, as long as you keep believing and working on it. In this way, you truly embrace the future—not as something to dread, but as an unfolding journey where even the hard parts serve a beautiful purpose.

Pain-to-Power Exercises – Chapter 12

1. Future Resilient Self Visualization: Find a quiet space and set aside fifteen minutes. Close your eyes and take several deep breaths. Then imagine yourself five years in the future, having continued developing your resilience. Visualize yourself facing a challenge with the wisdom, skills, and perspective you've been cultivating. Notice how you respond in this future—what thoughts arise, what actions you take, who you turn to for support. After exploring this vision, write a letter from your future self to your current self, offering guidance about a current challenge you're facing. This exercise helps you access the intuitive wisdom you already possess and creates a compelling vision of your developing resilience that can guide your growth.

2. Resilience Legacy Planning: Consider what wisdom about transforming pain into strength you would most want to pass on to others. Create a *resilience legacy plan* by addressing the following questions: What are the three to five most important insights about resilience I've gained through my own challenges? What specific practices have most helped me transform difficulty into growth? Who specifically might benefit from this wisdom, and what format would reach them effectively? Based on your answers, identify one specific action you'll take in the next month to begin sharing this wisdom. This exercise transforms your hard-won resilience insights from personal assets into contributions that might help others, adding another layer of meaning to your own struggles.

3. Resilience Rhythm Development: Create a sustainable pattern for ongoing resilience practice by establishing the following:

- Daily anchors: Identify two small daily practices requiring five minutes or less that support your resilience foundation.
- Weekly integration: Create a weekly ritual of fifteen to thirty minutes for deeper resilience reflection.

- Seasonal renewal: Plan quarterly *resilience renewal* experiences that allow deeper reflection and recalibration.

This layered approach creates a sustainable rhythm that builds resilience continuously rather than just during crises, weaving resilience practices into the fabric of everyday life so they become part of your identity rather than something you struggle to maintain.

As our journey together nears its end, we arrive at the ultimate truth about transforming pain into power: this work is never truly finished but becomes an integrated part of how we approach life's continuing challenges. The conclusion offers final reflections on embracing your innate capacity for resilience while acknowledging both the beauty and difficulty of this lifelong practice. The path forward remains yours to walk, strengthened by the insights and practices we've explored together.

CONCLUSION

A Call to Embrace Your Power

As I write these final words from my American home, my mind returns to that day in Caracas when a bomb shattered my car. Glass broke, smoke stung, and my old life ended—memories still sharp. Yet what threatened to destroy me ultimately transformed me. The bomb that nearly took my life ignited something far more powerful within—a force of resilience and innovation that redefined what was possible. Pain, which once threatened to destroy everything I held dear, became the sublime catalyst for a transformation I could never have imagined as I fled with nothing but a suitcase and my family.

This transformation—from devastation to strength, from victim to creator, from pain to empowerment—represents the magnificent journey we've explored together throughout this book. We've examined how suffering, while never something we would choose, inevitably becomes a doorway to unparalleled wisdom, resilience, and meaning when approached with intention. The human spirit possesses a boundless capacity to not merely survive difficulty but to be fundamentally transformed by it, always in ways that leave us stronger, more compassionate, and more purposeful than before.

The Paradox Revisited: Pain as a Portal to Power

Throughout human history, across cultures and wisdom traditions, a striking paradox appears: our greatest suffering invariably becomes the birthplace of our greatest strength. This paradox challenges our natural instinct to avoid pain at all costs. It proclaims that while suffering itself is not good, our response to it can transform it into something profoundly valuable. Pain, when engaged courageously and consciously, becomes not a dead end but a portal—a doorway to dimensions of human capacity and experience we might never otherwise discover.

We saw this paradox embodied in remarkable individuals like Viktor Frankl, who discovered meaning within the horrors of Nazi concentration camps, and Malala Yousafzai, whose near-fatal shooting catalyzed rather than silenced her advocacy. We encountered it in the scientific research on post-traumatic growth, showing how adversity consistently awakens latent strengths.

My own journey embodies this same paradox. The persecution that drove me from my homeland created unimaginable pain. Yet within that pain lay hidden gifts I could never have anticipated: appreciation for freedom, capacity to help others through similar transitions, clarity about my life's purpose, and resilience I never knew I possessed.

Throughout this book, we've explored specific approaches that facilitate this transformation:

- **Mindful awareness:** The practice of observing our pain with compassionate attention rather than either denying it or being consumed by it. This creates the space in which transformation becomes possible.
- **Meaning making:** The cognitive and spiritual work of finding purpose within suffering, connecting it to our values and larger life narrative. For me, this meant recognizing that my exile wasn't merely personal misfortune but part of a larger story of standing for freedom and truth against oppression.
- **Connection:** The healing power of authentic relationships during difficulty, allowing others to witness our struggle while receiving their

support. The community of fellow exiles became my lifeline, people who understood exactly what I had lost because they had lost it too.

- **Growth mindset:** The perspective that sees challenges as opportunities for development rather than merely threats to avoid. When I faced building a new career in a foreign language and culture, reframing these obstacles as chances to develop new capabilities made them manageable.

- **Action:** The transformative effect of converting pain into purposeful doing rather than passive enduring. Creating DolarToday to provide censored financial information to my countrymen gave my suffering direction and impact.

These approaches don't eliminate pain, but they transform our relationship with it. They convert what might be merely destructive suffering into a catalyst for growth—a painful but productive passage into greater wisdom, strength, and purpose.

As Viktor Frankl observed, "When we are no longer able to change a situation, we are challenged to change ourselves." This insight captures the essence of the pain-to-power journey. We may not choose the difficulties that befall us, but we retain the freedom to choose our response to them. In that response lies our greatest power.

The Kintsugi Life: Beauty in the Broken Places

In traditional Japanese aesthetics, there exists a practice called *kintsugi*—the art of repairing broken pottery with gold. Rather than hiding the damage, kintsugi artisans highlight the cracks, filling them with precious metal to create something more beautiful and valuable than the original unbroken piece. The philosophy behind this practice suggests that breakage and repair become part of an object's history, something to illuminate rather than conceal.

This ancient art form offers a sublime metaphor for the human journey through suffering to strength. When life breaks us—through loss, trauma, failure, or other painful experiences—we face a choice. We can try to hide the damage, cre-

181

ating a facade of wholeness that denies our wounds. We can leave the pieces shattered, defining ourselves primarily by our brokenness. Or we can engage in a kind of personal kintsugi—a transformative integration that honors the reality of our suffering while creating something radiantly beautiful from it.

I see this kintsugi reality in my own life. The fracture lines of my exile from my native land, filled with the gold of purpose and perspective, have created something different than what existed before—neither the unblemished original nor merely damaged goods, but a new integration that contains both genuine loss and transcendent beauty. The painful ruptures in my life story became, through conscious engagement, the very features that now give it unmatched character and meaning.

Living a kintsugi life involves several key elements:

- **Honest acknowledgment:** The art begins with recognizing actual breakage rather than pretending wholeness where wounds exist. Genuine integration requires acknowledging real pain rather than glossing over it with premature positivity.
- **Careful tending:** Kintsugi requires patient, skillful repair. Similarly, transforming personal suffering into strength demands masterful engagement rather than haphazard processing.
- **Artistic vision:** The kintsugi master sees broken pottery not merely as damaged goods but as material for a new creation that honors both the original form and the reality of breakage.
- **Generous sharing:** Completed kintsugi pieces don't hide in shame but offer their distinctive beauty to observers. Similarly, those who have transformed personal suffering into strength often discover that their integrated stories become priceless gifts to others.

As you reflect on your own life, consider this: What broken places might be waiting for the gold of conscious integration? What cracks in your story could potentially become the very features that make it uniquely meaningful and beautiful?

Final Call to Action: Transform Your Pain into Unstoppable Power

As you close these pages, remember that the story is now yours to continue. *The Power of Pain* is not just a concept for others in anecdotes and research; it is a vibrant, living potential in your own heart and mind. You have the tools in your toolkit—from mindfulness to reframing to seeking meaning and beyond. You have inspiration from those who've walked through fire and emerged shining. And most importantly, you have survived your own challenges and are still here, reading this, stronger than perhaps you give yourself credit for.

Now is the time to embrace your suffering—past, present, and future—not as a curse, but as a kind of dark soil in which the flowers of strength and character can gloriously bloom. This is not to glorify pain; it is to reclaim your narrative from pain. You are not simply a product of what has happened to you; you are, above all, a product of how you have decided to respond.

By embracing your suffering, you not only change your own life, but you contribute to a more resilient world. Your family, your community, and even strangers can be touched by the example of someone who lives with what I call "open-armed resilience"—someone who doesn't shrink from life's experiences but embraces them, however prickly they may be, trusting that they can be turned into something valuable.

In my own journey, from Venezuela to exile, from being silenced to speaking out, from the depths of doubt to renewed purpose, I have learned one overarching truth: the human spirit is infinitely powerful. The very fact that you've made it to this point testifies to your unassailable resilience.

Let your pain be your ally. Let it remind you of what matters, let it connect you with others, and let it drive you to make changes in yourself or the world that are needed. When you face new pain, remember all the pain you've already survived—a reservoir of resilience resides in you from those experiences.

As we part, I leave you with a final image: your scars are stripes of gold. They are not ugly marks to hide; they are proof of your healing, your history, and your strength.

Your pain is the breaking of the shell that encloses your understanding. Within that opening, your strength is born. Step forward and claim it.

Pain-to-Power Exercises – Final Reflection

1. Personal Practice Assessment: Take time to reflect honestly on how you currently respond to pain and difficulty. Create three columns on paper: "What Works For Me," "What Doesn't Work," and "What I Want To Try." In the first column, list approaches from this book that immediately resonated or practices you already use successfully. In the second, note approaches that felt forced or unhelpful when you've tried them. In the third, identify two to three new practices you're most curious to explore. This personalized assessment becomes your roadmap for developing sustainable resilience practices aligned with your unique needs and preferences rather than trying to force techniques that don't fit your temperament or circumstances.

2. Resilience Touchstone Creation: Develop a physical or digital touchstone that embodies your commitment to transforming pain into power. This might be a written personal resilience creed or manifesto, a visual collage of images representing your growth journey, a small object you carry that symbolizes your resilience, a carefully chosen quote or mantra stored in your phone, or a melody or song that reconnects you to your strength. Your touchstone serves as an immediate anchor during difficult moments, bypassing intellectual analysis and creating an embodied reminder of your capacity for transformation. Share what you've created with someone you trust, explaining its significance to deepen your own connection to its meaning.

3. Legacy of Resilience: Imagine you've been asked to write a short letter to someone facing a challenge similar to one you've overcome. What wisdom would you share? What specific practices helped you most? What perspective shifts made the biggest difference? Write this letter—even if you have no specific recipient in mind yet. The act of articulating your hard-won insights not only clarifies them for others but deepens your own integration of these principles. Many find that in teaching others about resilience, they strengthen their own capacity. Consider whether there's someone in your life who might benefit from receiving your letter, or save it for a future moment when you encounter someone who needs exactly the wisdom you've gained.

Remember that these exercises, like all practices we've explored, aren't about perfection but about progress. The goal isn't flawless implementation, but genuine engagement with your own Thank you for reading, and I wish you a life of growth, purpose, and the unshakable knowledge that your greatest strength will rise from your greatest challenges.

Go forth and turn your pain into power!

—Ivan D. Lozada

The PowerPain App — A Digital Companion

Bridging Knowledge and Practice in Your Resilience Journey

Throughout this book, we've explored the art of transforming suffering into strength. The principles and practices we've discussed have the power to radically shift your relationship with pain—yet as many readers have shared with me, the real challenge often lies not in understanding these concepts but in applying them consistently, especially during life's most difficult moments.

In conversations with countless individuals navigating their own journeys of transformation, I repeatedly heard the same question: "How do I hold onto these principles when I'm in the middle of the storm?" This challenge—translating understanding into consistent action—inspired the creation of a digital companion to support your ongoing resilience practice.

From Personal Need to Supportive Tool

When I first arrived in America in 2005, rebuilding my life required consistent practice, even on days when grief felt overwhelming. Small daily habits—a moment of mindfulness, brief journaling, or remembering a resilience principle at the right moment—often made the difference between despair and forward movement.

Two decades later, as I was finishing this book in 2025, I realized that our phones are always within reach during life's most challenging moments. This insight led to the PowerPain app—a tool designed to transform the device we carry everywhere into a portable resilience companion that supports your practice whenever and wherever you need it most.

The paradox wasn't lost on me: after exploring digital overwhelm earlier in this book, I was now creating another digital tool. Yet this reflects a truth we've discovered throughout our journey—the problem isn't technology itself but how we engage with it. Just as pain becomes destructive or constructive depending on our response, technology can either fragment or focus us depending on our intentions and how we design our interactions with it.

Embodying the Book's Principles

The PowerPain app was created as a practical extension of this book's core philosophy. Each feature embodies specific principles we've explored:

Personalized Approach

Just as each person's pain is unique, so, too, is their path to resilience. The app meets you where you are emotionally, offering practices tailored to your current state—whether you're feeling anxious, grieving, frustrated, or overwhelmed. For example, if you're experiencing anxiety, the app might offer a guided breathing exercise from chapter 6, while if you're feeling a sense of meaninglessness, it might present a meaning-making reflection from chapter 4 specifically adapted to your current emotional state.

Integration of Mind, Body, and Spirit

Drawing from the holistic approach we've explored, the app integrates cognitive reframing exercises, somatic awareness practices, and meaning-oriented reflections. This comprehensive approach honors the understanding that pain affects us across multiple dimensions and true resilience requires addressing all aspects of our experience.

Balance of Structure and Flexibility

The app offers both guided pathways for those seeking clear direction and exploratory options for those who prefer self-direction. This balance reflects our understanding that resilience development requires both structured practice and intuitive adaptation to your unique needs.

Community Connection

Honoring the vital role of connection we discussed in chapter 6, the app includes optional community features that connect you with others on similar journeys. These connections embody our understanding that while transformation is deeply personal, it flourishes within supportive relationships.

Features That Support Your Practice

The PowerPain app includes several elements designed to bridge the gap between understanding and consistent practice:

- **Micro-practices for daily life:** Recognizing that transformation happens through consistent small actions rather than occasional grand gestures, the app offers brief resilience-building exercises that take just one to three minutes. For instance, you might receive a targeted reframing exercise from chapter 6 when you need it most, or a "Witness Practice" from chapter 8 adapted to fit into a busy schedule.
- **Contextual reminders:** Based on your settings and schedule, the app can deliver timely resilience principles before difficult meetings, during commutes, or at personally significant times—providing the right wisdom at moments when you're most likely to need support.
- **Digital journaling with reflection prompts:** The app gives you a private journaling space to process your pain, track insights, and document your growth. The digital format means you'll always have it with you so you can capture thoughts in the moment and witness your developing resilience over time. The prompts are based directly on the Pain-to-Power exercises from each chapter, tailored to your current emotional state.

- **Guided practices:** Meditations and reflective exercises specifically designed for different forms of suffering—from acute grief to chronic stress to identity challenges—provide evidence-based approaches for shifting your relationship with pain.

- **Progress visualization:** While transformation isn't linear, seeing patterns over time provides valuable feedback on your developing resilience. Visual representations of your practice consistency and emerging insights give you visible evidence of your progress.

Balanced Technology Use

Consistent with the digital mindfulness we explored in chapter 11, the PowerPain app was designed with a clear awareness of technology's potential pitfalls:

- **Purposeful engagement:** Unlike platforms designed to maximize screen time, PowerPain encourages brief, intentional interactions followed by returning to present-moment awareness. The app even acknowledges when you close it after completing a practice.

- **Offline functionality:** All core features function without internet connection, ensuring support even when disconnected.

- **Physical world integration:** Many exercises deliberately guide you back to your physical environment, sensory experience, and in-person relationships rather than keeping your attention on the screen.

- **Respect for attention boundaries:** Unlike many apps that interrupt with notifications, PowerPain functions primarily when you choose to open it, with optional notifications that respect your attention boundaries.

These design choices reflect a fundamental principle: digital tools should serve our humanity rather than diminish it. The app aims to strengthen your innate capacity for resilience, not create dependence on external solutions.

Your Path Forward

Whether you choose to incorporate digital support into your practice or prefer traditional methods like handwritten journals, in-person groups, or established spiritual practices, the key is finding sustainable routines that work for your life. Transformation isn't about perfectly implementing every principle we've discussed, but about gradually integrating these approaches into your natural responses to life's challenges.

You may find a digital companion invaluable, or you may prefer analog methods. Some will benefit from community support; others will pursue a more solitary path. Some will engage most deeply with mindfulness practices; others will connect more with meaning making or creative expression. The path from pain to power has many routes, and the wisest approach is finding what resonates most deeply with your unique needs and circumstances.

If you're interested in exploring the PowerPain app as a companion to your resilience practice, you can find more information at **www.powerpain.org**. The app is currently under development and will be available for both iOS and Android devices upon launch, with both free and premium options to support different needs and preferences.

The PowerPain app directly implements the key resilience principles explored throughout this book: mindfulness practices from chapter 6, cognitive reframing techniques from chapter 4, meaning-making exercises from chapter 3, and the embodied approaches discussed in chapter 8. Each feature was designed to translate these evidence-based concepts into daily practice, creating a seamless bridge between understanding resilience principles and living them consistently. Whether through guided journaling that echoes the Pain-to-Power exercises from each chapter or micro-meditations that build the presence skills we explored in chapter 6, the app serves as a practical extension of the book's methodology.

Remember that whether digital or analog, the most powerful tool for transformation remains your own intention and awareness. No app, book, or program can do the inner work for you—but the right support can make that work more consistent, accessible, and ultimately effective in your ongoing journey from pain to power.

32873561R00110